FITWAFFLE'S
Baking It Easy

ALL MY BEST 3-INGREDIENT RECIPES *and* MOST-LOVED CAKES *and* DESSERTS

Eloise Head

weldon**owen**

The prettiest cupcakes

Contents

Welcome to my first ever baking book

Whether you are totally new to baking or have been baking for years, I hope this book brings you joy, gives you inspiration and allows you to make some absolutely delicious bakes.

As you can tell from the title, every recipe in this book is designed to be easy. Baking doesn't have to be complicated; you don't have to be an expert, and you don't have to use fancy ingredients if you don't want to. Baking should be fun, relaxing and a little messy.

In this book, you will find a collection of my best **3-ingredient**, **4-ingredient** and **5-ingredient** recipes, plus some of my ultimate favorites that I just couldn't leave out. All your favorite flavors are here – cookies and cream, speculoos, chocolate-hazelnut, different types of chocolate, salted caramel, peanut butter, cinnamon and more.

Thank you to all my amazing followers and supporters for making this possible. I hope you love this book as much as I loved writing it for you.

Turn over to find out more about me and my story...

ABOUT ME

Eloise Head

What's up, guys! I'm Eloise, the face and name behind Fitwaffle. I'm a total food lover with a huge sweet tooth. I absolutely love being in the kitchen, trying new foods and creating easy and exciting recipes. I've loved baking ever since I was a child, so this book is just a dream come true for me, and I am SO excited to be able to share it with you.

Let me start by telling you a little bit about how I came up with Fitwaffle, as I think it's a good place to begin. The name combines my two passions: fitness and food. The 'waffle' part also refers to talking (waffling on), as I tend to do a lot of that, too!

Before Fitwaffle became my full-time job, I worked in the fitness industry, first as a personal trainer then as a manager of a fitness center. Ever since I was tiny, I have always been super active and sporty and I loved dance. My mum and dad would tell you that I never sat still. They would also tell you that I've always had a sweet tooth and loved cake, sweets and all things indulgent, so not much has changed. My great-auntie was an amazing cook. My sister and I would frequently visit and she would teach us how to make jam tarts, fairy cakes, iced cookies, cheese scones and more. I think this is where my love of baking began.

Unfortunately, I haven't always had a good relationship with food. When I was 18 years old, I became overly obsessed with working out, doing fitness classes and spending hours at the gym. I also started 'eating clean,' meaning I cut out just about every processed food from my diet, including cake, chocolate, fast food and even white potatoes (all the things I really enjoyed). I lost a lot of weight, including a lot of muscle. I had endless fights with my mum and I had a very unhealthy mindset regarding food. I considered certain items to be 'good' and others to be 'bad,' with no real knowledge about nutrition or how any of these foods actually affected my body.

Fast forward a year, and I enrolled in a year-long personal training course. I learned about anatomy, resistance training and nutrition. Most importantly, I learned more about macronutrients: protein, fats and carbs, which make up all foods. This new knowledge completely changed how I looked at food, which I no longer saw as 'good' or 'bad.' I was now able to regard what I ate for what it was without any emotional attachments or labels. I learned that, at the end of the day, food is energy. Some foods are high in calories and low in nutrients, while others are low in calories and high in nutrients. It's the balance of these foods that matters, alongside your personal energy output.

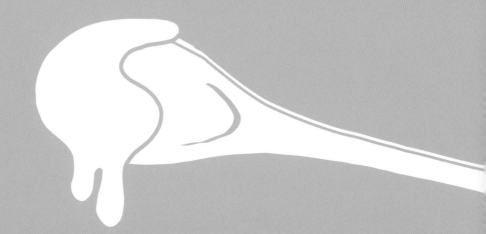

For the past seven years, with some hiccups along the way, I've eaten all foods in moderation and learned to enjoy my old favorites again. This is what sparked Fitwaffle, which began as an Instagram page and online blog documenting my fitness and food journey. I would work as a personal trainer in the week, then visit London on the weekends with my fiancé to snap pictures of incredible burgers and work through the list of restaurants and street food we wanted to try.

When the coronavirus pandemic put the nation into lockdown, restaurants closed and we were all advised to stay home. I started posting my homemade creations and recipes to my Instagram page and TikTok. This is also when I created the page @FitwaffleKitchen. I got to work in my tiny one-bedroom flat, using some laminated floorboards on my kitchen table as a backdrop and a homemade stand to hold my phone while I was filming. I wanted to build a community of fellow bakers and foodies in a time of uncertainty where we all felt isolated. I made it my personal mission to help keep people occupied and uplifted during these difficult times. I also wanted to make sure that my recipes were accessible to as many people as possible – that they were easy and achievable, without all the fluff.

I posted many 3-, 4- and 5-ingredient recipes with products you could actually get hold of during lockdown, when flour was like gold dust! Roll on a couple years to now, and I can't believe I'm sitting here writing my own book. Thanks to all my INCREDIBLE followers, your amazing support and unbelievably inspirational messages, I now get to share it with you, and I honestly cannot thank you enough.

As you go through the book, you will notice each chapter starts with 3-ingredient recipes, then progresses on to those with 4 and 5 ingredients. The All-Star Bakes, as I like to call them, can be found together in the final chapter. They're a little more complex and use more ingredients, but they are so popular and delicious, it would have been a shame to leave them out.

The recipes include fan favorites from my Instagram page, TikTok and YouTube channel, plus some totally new ones that I know you will absolutely love. Look out for the option to 'swap' ingredients in recipes. For example, if you don't like peanut butter or don't have chocolate spread in the house, you can swap it for something else to suit your taste buds.

Happy baking everybody! Enjoy x

GETTING STARTED

~

All my tips

USEFUL EQUIPMENT

- ☐ Large, medium and small mixing bowls
- ☐ 8 x 8 x 1.5 in (20 x 20 x 4cm) square baking pan
- ☐ 8in (20cm) round springform cake pan
- ☐ 8 x 10 x 1.5 in (20 x 25 x 4cm) baking pan
- ☐ 6-cup and 12-cup muffin pans
- ☐ Loaf pans
- ☐ Cupcake and muffin liners
- ☐ Parchment paper
- ☐ Electric hand mixer
- ☐ Balloon whisk
- ☐ Wooden mixing spoons

- ☐ Rubber spatulas
- ☐ Weighing scales
- ☐ Measuring spoons
- ☐ Oven thermometer
- ☐ Sieve
- ☐ Food processor/blender
- ☐ Ice cream scoop/ cookie scoop
- ☐ Plastic wrap
- ☐ Large saucepan
- ☐ Large frying pan
- ☐ Large nonstick cookie sheets or sheet pans
- ☐ Sugar thermometer

THINGS I WISH I'D KNOWN BEFORE I STARTED BAKING

Thank me later

• Every oven is different. While some are conventional electric ovens, some have fans (otherwise known as convection ovens) and others are gas-heated. The better you get to know your oven, the more consistent your baking will become. You can't always trust the dial on your cooker, which is why I recommend using a separate oven thermometer. It's great to have peace of mind that you are cooking at the right temperature.

• Place your bake in the center of the oven, on the middle rack. This will help it to cook more evenly. If your oven tends to be hotter on one side, like mine is, you can carefully rotate the bake using oven mitts partway through to ensure even cooking. This doesn't apply to cakes, as you should never open the oven while cakes are baking.

• Pan sizes can have a big impact on the speed of baking. If you are using a pan that isn't the specified size for the recipe, you will need to adjust the cooking time. Larger pans = shallower bakes, meaning they will cook quicker. Smaller pans = deeper bakes, meaning they will take longer to cook.

• When making cookies, a large nonstick cookie sheet is your best friend. They don't need lining with parchment paper and the cookies won't stick! If you don't have a cookie sheet, make sure to use a large sheet pan and line it with parchment paper to stop your cookies from sticking to the sheet pan.

• Some of these recipes will need you to warm a knife. The best way to do this is to fill a tall, sturdy glass or jug with hot water (enough to cover the blade), then place the knife in the water for 5 minutes before using.

• All microwave instructions in this book are based on a 700W microwave. If your microwave is more powerful, set it to medium-high or medium and check the bake before the stated time, as it may already be cooked.

MY INGREDIENT TIPS FOR THE BEST BAKES

1
EGGS

It's always best to use room-temperature eggs in cake batters, blondies and brownies, as they will blend more evenly into your batter and will help your cakes to rise more easily. Cold eggs can make your batter lumpy.

2
MILK

As with eggs, using room-temperature milk will blend more easily into the other ingredients, giving a nice smooth batter. It can also help the bake to cook more quickly and evenly.

3
FOOD COLORING

When using food coloring, I would strongly recommend using a high-quality brand, such as Sugarflair or Wilton. Supermarket food colorings are generally not strong enough, and using too much in order to get your desired color can ruin the consistency of the bake.

4
CREAMS

Use good-quality full-fat cream cheese (I use Philadelphia) and pour off any excess liquid before using. When making cheesecakes, make sure your cream cheese is at room temperature, as this will help the ingredients to blend more easily, creating a firmer cheesecake.

When whipping heavy cream to stiff peaks, make sure the cream is cold, as warm cream will not form stiff peaks. The colder the cream, the better and quicker it will whip. You can also refrigerate your bowl and beaters to speed things up and help the cream stay cool for longer.

MOST-USED INGREDIENTS

As well as the baking standards – eggs, butter, flour, baking powder, sugar and milk – these are the ingredients I use most often in my recipes. Turn the page to see some of them pictured. Any brand will do but I have mentioned my favorites below.

- [ ] Cream-filled chocolate sandwich cookies (I like Oreos)
- [ ] Speculoos cookies and spread/cookie butter (I like Biscoff)
- [ ] Chocolate-hazelnut spread (I like Nutella)
- [ ] Creamy peanut butter
- [ ] Ground cinnamon
- [ ] Caramel filling (I like Carnation)
- [ ] Ripe bananas
- [ ] Condensed milk
- [ ] White chocolate
- [ ] Milk chocolate
- [ ] Dark chocolate (at least 50% cocoa/cacao)

- [ ] Full-fat cream cheese
- [ ] Chocolate chips (dark, milk and white)
- [ ] Chocolate bars (I like Snickers and Twix) and peanut butter cups (such as Reese's), standard and mini
- [ ] Marshmallows, standard and mini
- [ ] Puffed rice cereal and cornflakes
- [ ] Heavy cream
- [ ] Graham crackers
- [ ] Apples – Granny Smiths are great for baking
- [ ] Cooking oil spray

Caramel filling

Chocolate-hazelnut
spread

Condensed
milk

Marshmallows

Cream-filled
chocolate
sandwich
cookies

Puffed rice cereal
and cornflakes

Speculoos cookies
and smooth
speculoos spread

Peanut
butter

White and
milk chocolate

Bananas

HOW TO...
MY MOST-ASKED QUESTIONS

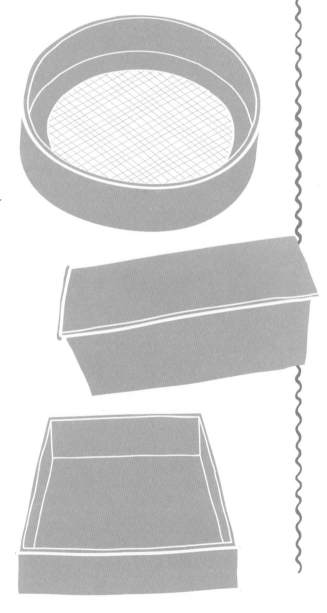

... Line your pans

This is one of the things that I get asked the most on social media: how do I line my pans and what parchment paper do I use? I would recommend using Reynolds Kitchens Parchment Paper, as it's really thick and holds its shape, and this is how I use it:

- **To line your square or rectangular baking pans**, use two pans of the same size. Measure a piece of parchment paper over one of the pans so it has about a 4in (10cm) overhang all the way around the edge. Using the second pan, press the parchment paper down into the first pan, then fold the overhang down over the edges, making sure to create sharp creases in the pan so the lining paper holds its shape and is a really snug fit.

- **Lining the bottom of round springform cake pans** makes it easier to remove your cooled or chilled bakes. To do this, place a sheet of parchment paper on a chopping board or similar, then place the base of your cake pan on top. With the tip of a sharp knife, 'draw' around the cake pan – you should cut through the paper just enough so that you can press out the circle. Alternatively, grab a pencil and trace around the outside of your cake pan, then cut along the inside the line with scissors. The best way to remove a cake or cheesecake from the pan is to run a sharp knife carefully around the inside of the pan, then unclip it, open the ring and slowly lift it over the cake. Now remove the cake or cheesecake from the pan base, peeling off the lining paper.

... Heat-treat flour

When using flour in no-bake recipes and mug cakes, it's best to heat-treat the flour first. This is because raw flour can contain bacteria that may be harmful. Better to be safe than sorry...

- **In the microwave** Put the flour onto a microwave-safe plate and microwave on a medium-high setting for about 90 seconds, stirring every 20 seconds, until the flour is hot throughout. Leave to cool to room temperature before use.

- **In the oven** Preheat the oven to 340°F/170°C (150°C fan)/Gas mark 3½. Spread the flour evenly on a sheet pan and heat in the oven for about 5 minutes, carefully removing it and stirring every couple of minutes, until the flour is hot throughout. Leave to cool to room temperature before use.

- **In a pan** Put the flour into a heavy frying pan and warm over a medium heat for 4–4½ minutes, stirring to ensure the flour doesn't burn on the bottom of the pan, until it is hot throughout. Leave to cool to room temperature before use.

... Melt chocolate

First, break the chocolate into about scant ½in (1cm) pieces.

- **In the microwave** Put the chocolate pieces into a microwave-safe bowl and microwave on a medium-high setting in 30-second bursts, stirring at each interval. When the chocolate has almost fully melted, continue to stir it with a spoon until all the lumps have disappeared and the chocolate is runny and smooth.

- **In a double boiler** Make sure you have a saucepan and a large heatproof bowl (I recommend glass) that sits about halfway into your pan. Fill the saucepan with about 2in (5cm) of water. Put your chocolate pieces in the bowl, then sit it on top of the saucepan and turn on the stove so the water starts to simmer. As the water heats up and steam is released, the steam stays trapped between the bowl and the pan, which then heats and melts the chocolate. As this happens, gently stir the chocolate until it's runny and smooth.

FUDGE, CUPS, TRUFFLES and BITES

~~~

Chapter One

Fun, super quick and easy to make...

These are the recipes that really kicked off my obsession for baking and were an absolute lifesaver for me and a lot of my followers during the first lockdown. I just love how fun, quick and easy they are to make – plus, for most of them, there's no 'real' baking involved. Just grab a saucepan and a mixing bowl, and you're pretty much ready to go – great when you're short on time or don't want to turn the oven on! They're also perfect for sharing and great to bring to parties.

In this chapter, you will find some of my most popular recipes EVER, including 3-ingredient **Cookies and Cream Fudge**, **Cookies and Cream Truffles**, **Honeycomb**, plus my 4-ingredient **Speculoos Cups**. Yum!

Don't be afraid to get a little messy and experiment with flavors here. These recipes are the ultimate boredom-killers – and, of course, they taste great!

One of my favorites

STUFFED COOKIE CUPS

Makes 6

Soft and warm chocolate chip cookie dough, stuffed with your favorite chocolate! These little cups are so easy to make and they're super versatile to suit your taste. Stuff them with cream-filled chocolate sandwich cookies, peanut butter cups, toffee-filled chocolates or even a blob of chocolate spread.

25 minutes

12.4oz (350g) pack ready-to-bake chocolate chip cookie dough

6 chocolates chocolate candies or cookies of your choice

01 Preheat the oven to 400°F/200°C (180°C fan)/Gas mark 6 and line a 6-cup muffin pan with cupcake liners. Alternatively, if you have one, spray the cups of a silicone muffin mold with cooking oil.

02 Divide the cookie dough into 12 small pieces, then press 1 of the pieces into the bottom of a cupcake liner. Repeat with another 5 pieces of the dough to fill each liner.

03 Place 1 chocolate or cookie in each liner, then gently press another piece of cookie dough on top of each one, making sure the edges are sealed and none of the filling is visible.

04 Bake for 12–15 minutes until golden brown and the cookie dough is cooked through. Leave to cool in the pan for 15 minutes, then transfer to a cooling rack to cool completely. Enjoy!

05 Store in an airtight container for up to 4 days.

TIP:

Feel free to make your own cookie dough using the recipe on page 241.

CHOCOLATE CARAMEL FUDGE

Makes 64 pieces

〜

This fudge is super easy to make and very versatile. The chocolate-covered caramel cups melt into the warm mixture to create gooey caramel-and-chocolate swirls. It tastes just as good as it looks!

10 minutes
+ 3–4 hours chilling

1 x 13.4oz (380g) can dulce de leche
1lb (500g) white chocolate, broken into pieces
12oz (330g) chocolate-covered caramel cups (I use Rolos)

01 Line an 8in (20cm) square baking pan with parchment paper (see page 16).

02 Put the dulce de leche and white chocolate into a large saucepan and warm over a low–medium heat, stirring constantly with a wooden spoon, until the chocolate has melted and the mixture is thick and smooth. It should peel away from the bottom and sides of the pan when you stir the mixture or tilt the pan. If it still looks runny, continue to cook until it thickens.

03 Turn off the heat and add the chocolate-covered caramel cups, reserving 10–15 for the top. Fold in just a few times to avoid completely melting the chocolate, then pour the mixture into your prepared pan and smooth it out to the edges. Press the reserved chocolates into the top of the fudge.

04 Chill in the refrigerator for 3–4 hours until set, then cut into 64 x 1in (2.5cm) squares. Enjoy!

05 Store in an airtight container in the fridge for up to 5 days.

SWAP:

〜

Swap the chocolate-covered caramel cups for a different kind of chopped-up chocolate bar.

Fudge, Cups, Truffles & Bites

COOKIES and CREAM FUDGE

Makes 64 pieces

This creamy white chocolate fudge is sweet, delicious, and packed with cream-filled chocolate sandwich cookies. It was one of the first 3-ingredient recipes I ever made – in lockdown, when the shops were running out of many products. Luckily, white chocolate, condensed milk and cookies were still in stock! It is still my most popular recipe on Instagram. It doesn't require flour or butter, and no baking is involved, so it's the perfect speedy dessert and one to save for emergencies. These little pieces also make fab gifts or party snacks.

*10 minutes
+ 3-4 hours chilling*

1 x 14oz (397g) can
   condensed milk
1lb (500g) white chocolate,
   broken into pieces
20 cream-filled chocolate
sandwich cookies (I use
Oreos), roughly chopped

01 Line an 8in (20cm) square baking pan with parchment paper (see page 16).

02 Put the condensed milk and chocolate into a large saucepan and warm over a low–medium heat, stirring constantly with a wooden spoon, until the chocolate has melted and the mixture is thick and smooth. It should peel away from the bottom and sides of the pan when you stir the mixture or tilt the pan. If it still looks runny, continue to cook until it thickens.

03 Turn off the heat and fold in the chopped cookies (saving a handful for the top). Pour the mixture into your prepared pan and smooth it out to the edges. Scatter the remaining cookie pieces on top.

04 Chill in the refrigerator for 3–4 hours until set, then cut into 64 x 1in (2.5cm) squares. Enjoy!

05 Store in an airtight container in the fridge for up to 5 days.

EASTER FUDGE

Makes 64 pieces

~~

This fudge is sweet, creamy and perfect for Easter. It's packed with mini chocolate eggs, meaning your sweet tooth is sure to be satisfied, and it's fab for bringing to parties, or bag up and put in an Easter basket as a gift.

10 minutes
+ 3-4 hours chilling

6oz (180g) mini chocolate eggs (I use Cadbury Mini Eggs)
1 x 14oz (397g) can condensed milk
1lb (500g) white chocolate, broken into pieces

01 Line an 8in (20cm) square baking pan with parchment paper (see page 16).

02 Place half of the chocolate eggs on a chopping board and roughly crush with the end of a rolling pin or the back of a spoon.

03 Put the condensed milk and white chocolate into a large saucepan and warm over a low–medium heat, stirring constantly with a wooden spoon, until the chocolate has melted and the mixture is thick and smooth. It should peel away from the bottom and sides of the pan when you stir the mixture or tilt the pan. If it still looks runny, continue to cook until it thickens.

04 Turn off the heat and fold in the crushed chocolate eggs. Pour the mixture into your prepared pan and smooth it out to the edges. Press the remaining mini chocolate eggs into the top of the fudge.

05 Chill in the refrigerator for 3–4 hours until set, then cut into 64 x 1in (2.5cm) pieces. Enjoy!

06 Store in an airtight container in the fridge for up to 5 days.

SWAP:

~~

Try other types of chocolate eggs (I like using fondant-filled eggs, such as Cadbury Creme Eggs).

CRISPY CHOCOLATE FUDGE CUPS

Makes 12

~~

These chocolatey cups are creamy, fudgy and delicious, with a lovely crunch from the puffed rice cereal. They're super quick and easy to make, and you only need a microwave and one bowl – so barely any washing up. Winner!

5 minutes
+ 20 minutes chilling

1 cup (300g) chocolate
   spread
3½ tbsp (50g) coconut oil
⅓ cup (15g) puffed rice
   cereal (I use Rice Krispies)

01   Line a 12-cup muffin pan with cupcake liners.

02   Put the chocolate spread and coconut oil into a medium microwave-safe bowl and microwave on high in 30-second bursts, stirring at each interval, until melted and smooth.

03   Stir the puffed rice into the chocolate mixture, making sure it is fully coated, then spoon into your cupcake liners. Pop into the freezer and chill for about 20 minutes until hardened.

04   Store in an airtight container in the refrigerator for 3–4 days or in the freezer for up to 3 months.

Fudge, Cups, Truffles & Bites

SWAP:

~~

Swap the puffed rice with crushed cornflakes or any cereal of your choice.

PEANUT BUTTER CUPS

Makes 6

~~

You'll never have to leave the house again when you need a chocolate-and-peanut-butter fix! These homemade peanut butter cups are super quick and easy to make and totally irresistible. They're creamy, delicious and just melt in your mouth. Let's go!

*15 minutes
+ 1 hour 15 minutes
chilling*

10.5oz (300g) milk chocolate, broken into pieces and melted (see page 17)

Scant ½ cup (120g) creamy peanut butter

4 tbsp (30g) powdered sugar, sifted

01 Line a 6-cup muffin pan with cupcake liners.

02 Scoop 1 tablespoon of the melted chocolate into a cupcake liner and smooth it out, then use the back of a spoon to bring the chocolate about one third of the way up the sides of the liner. Repeat with more melted chocolate in the remaining liners, then pop into the refrigerator for 15 minutes while you make the peanut butter mix. Set aside the remaining melted chocolate.

03 Put the peanut butter and powdered sugar into a small bowl and mix together with a spoon until fully combined.

04 Remove the pan from the refrigerator, then scoop about 1 tablespoon of the peanut butter mixture into each chocolate cup and spread it out to the edges.

05 Top the cups with the remaining melted chocolate and smooth it out to the edges, making sure the peanut butter is completely covered. Chill in the refrigerator for 1 hour, then remove from the liners and enjoy!

06 Store in an airtight container in the refrigerator or at room temperature for up to 5 days.

SWAP:
~~
Replace the milk chocolate with white chocolate or dark chocolate to suit your taste buds.

COOKIES and CREAM TRUFFLES

Makes 9

These little truffles are the perfect dessert when you fancy something sweet and creamy but don't want to spend long in the kitchen. They taste like a super-delicious white chocolate cookies and cream cheesecake, but without the fuss and all the extra ingredients.

15 minutes + 1 hour chilling

9 cream-filled chocolate sandwich cookies (I use Oreos)
2oz (60g) full-fat cream cheese
5.25oz (150g) white chocolate, broken into pieces

Fudge, Cups, Truffles & Bites

01 Put the cookies into a food processor and process until finely crushed. Alternatively, put them into a plastic bag and crush with a rolling pin. Tip the crushed cookies into a medium bowl, reserving 1 tablespoon of the crumbs in a separate small bowl for later. Add the cream cheese and mix it in with a spoon until fully combined.

02 Scoop up about 1 tablespoon of the mixture, then roll into a ball with your hands and place on a freezer-proof plate. Repeat with the remaining mixture to make 9 truffles, then transfer to the freezer and chill for 30 minutes.

03 When ready to coat, set a cooling rack over a sheet of parchment paper and melt the chocolate (see page 17).

04 Using 2 forks, coat each ball in the melted chocolate, letting any excess drip off, then transfer to the prepared cooling rack and sprinkle over the reserved cookie crumbs.

05 Chill in the refrigerator for 30 minutes, or until set. Carefully pop them off the cooling rack (you don't want to crack the chocolate) and serve. Enjoy!

06 Store in an airtight container in the refrigerator for up to 4 days.

SWAP:

Use cream-filled vanilla sandwich cookies (I use Golden Oreos) and milk chocolate for a different look and taste.

GINGERBREAD TRUFFLES

Makes 9

~~

These truffles are perfect for Christmas, or whenever you want to enjoy gingerbread. The warming spices pair perfectly with the sweet, subtle white chocolate and cream cheese. They make fab mini Christmas desserts and will look amazing on the festive table. You won't be able to get enough of them!

15 minutes
+ 1 hour chilling

3.5oz (100g) gingerbread cookies

2oz (60g) full-fat cream cheese

5.25oz (150g) white chocolate, broken into pieces

01 Put the cookies into a food processor and process until finely crushed. Alternatively, put them into a plastic bag and crush with a rolling pin. Tip into a medium bowl, then stir in the cream cheese with a spoon until fully combined.

02 Scoop up about 1 tablespoon of the mixture, then roll into a ball with your hands and place on a freezer-proof plate. Repeat with the remaining mixture to make 9 truffles, then transfer to the freezer and chill for 30 minutes.

03 When ready to coat, set a cooling rack over a sheet of parchment paper and melt the chocolate (see page 17).

04 Using 2 forks, coat each ball in the melted chocolate, letting any excess drip off, then transfer to the prepared cooling rack.

05 Chill in the refrigerator for 30 minutes, or until set. Carefully pop them off the cooling rack (you don't want to crack the chocolate) and serve. Enjoy!

06 Store in an airtight container in the refrigerator for up to 4 days.

Optional decoration ~~~~~~~~~~~~~~~~~~~~~~~~

At Step 4, after coating the balls in the melted chocolate, decorate with festive sugar sprinkles and leave to set.

HOT CHOCOLATE TRUFFLES

Makes 12

If you love hot chocolate, this is the recipe for you. These truffles can be dropped into hot milk for the most luxurious, rich and creamy hot chocolate in the comfort of your own home! The best thing about the recipe is that you can make as many truffles as you like and store them in the freezer, ready to make an incredible hot chocolate at any time.

15 minutes
+ 3 hours 30 minutes chilling

1½ cups (350g) dark chocolate chips
Scant 1 cup (230ml) heavy cream
9oz (250g) milk chocolate, broken into pieces + a handful of milk chocolate shavings, to decorate

01 Put the chocolate chips and cream into a medium saucepan and warm over a low heat, stirring with a wooden spoon, until melted and smooth. Pour into a heatproof container and chill in the refrigerator for 2 hours.

02 Scoop up 2 tablespoons of the mixture and place on a freezer-proof plate in a round blob, then repeat with the remaining mixture to make 12, making sure the blobs don't touch each other. Transfer to the freezer and chill for 1 hour.

03 When ready to coat, set a cooling rack over a sheet of parchment paper and melt the milk chocolate (see page 17).

04 Remove the chocolate blobs from the freezer and roll into balls with your hands. Next, using 2 forks, coat each ball in the melted chocolate, letting any excess drip off, then transfer to the prepared cooling rack and sprinkle with the chocolate shavings to decorate.

05 Chill in the refrigerator for 30 minutes, or until set. Carefully pop them off the cooling rack (you don't want to crack the chocolate) and store in an airtight container in the freezer for up to 3 months.

Serving suggestion 〜〜〜〜〜〜〜〜〜〜〜〜〜〜〜

Drop 1 truffle into a mug of hot milk and stir until melted. If it takes a while to melt, pop the mug in the microwave for 30 seconds and stir until fully combined. And there you have it! A luxury hot chocolate at home.

TIP:
This recipe can easily be halved or doubled, depending on how many truffles you want to make.

Fudge, Cups, Truffles & Bites

PEANUT BUTTER S'MORES DIP

Serves 4-6

~

Warm, melted peanut butter and chocolate, with gooey toasted marshmallows – all the flavors of s'mores, but baked in the oven. It's so easy! Perfect for summer or winter, why not make it at a sleepover, for a movie night or after dinner with friends? It needs just two main ingredients, plus whatever you want to dip into it.

35 minutes

6oz (180g) mini peanut butter cups (I use Reese's)

2 cups (100g) mini marshmallows

Digestive biscuits or graham crackers, for dipping

01 Preheat the oven to 400°F/200°C (180°C fan)/Gas mark 6.

02 Put the peanut butter cups into an 7in (18cm) cast-iron skillet, or ovenproof frying pan or dish, and sprinkle the mini marshmallows on top.

03 Bake for 20–25 minutes until the marshmallows look melted, puffy and golden on top. Carefully remove from the oven and leave to cool for 5 minutes.

04 For a crispier top, place the dish under the broiler for 3–5 minutes until the top turns crisp and golden, then leave to cool for 5 minutes.

05 Dip your digestive biscuits or graham crackers into the gooey marshmallows and melted chocolate and enjoy. Absolutely delicious!

Fudge, Cups, Truffles & Bites

SWAP:
~

Swap peanut butter cups for chocolate chunks, and dip strawberries instead of the biscuits.

CHOCOLATE BARK

Makes 12 chunks

~~~

This is the ultimate gift for when you're short on time and energy, because there's no 'real' baking involved. It's super versatile to suit any taste buds, so go wild. You can use dark, milk or white chocolate as the base, then play around with the chocolate swirl and the toppings. It looks great bagged up with a little ribbon and can be customized for any event or special occasion. Have fun!

15 minutes
+ 2 hours setting

1lb (500g) milk chocolate or dark chocolate (at least 50% cocoa/cacao), broken into pieces

5.25oz (150g) white chocolate, broken into pieces

Chopped chocolate bars or broken cookies of your choice (see suggestions below)

01   Line a 13 x 9in (33 x 23cm) sheet pan with parchment paper.

02   Pop the milk or dark chocolate and white chocolate into separate microwave-safe bowls and melt in the microwave or in a double boiler (see page 17).

03   Pour your melted milk or dark chocolate into the prepared sheet pan and smooth it out gently with a metal spatula or the back of a spoon. Dollop on the melted white chocolate, then swirl it through the milk or dark chocolate base with a knife or skewer to create a pretty pattern.

04   Arrange your chosen topping(s) over the top, then leave to set at room temperature or in the refrigerator for about 2 hours. When set, cut or break into 12 chunks.

05   Store in an airtight container for up to 2 weeks.

Topping suggestions ~~~~~~~~~~~~~~~~~~~~~~

Try topping the chocolate with: candy-coated chocolate buttons (such as Smarties or M&Ms), cream-filled chocolate sandwich cookies (such as Oreos), pretzels, peanut butter cups, or caramel shortbread chocolate fingers (such as Twix).

POPCORN BALLS

Makes 8

These balls are great for sleepovers, movie nights and parties. They're super versatile, so perfect for all occasions – add red and green candy-coated chocolate buttons (like M&Ms) for Christmas, or pink food coloring for Valentine's Day, or why not pop them on a stick and cover them in chocolate? The options are endless!

15 minutes
+ 1-2 hours setting

1 x 1oz (30g) bag microwave popcorn, such as kettle corn

3 tbsp (45g) unsalted butter

8oz (225g) marshmallows

01   Prepare the popcorn according to the package directions.

02   Put the butter and marshmallows into a large saucepan and warm over a medium heat, stirring constantly with a wooden spoon, until melted. Remove from the heat and add the popcorn, stirring until it is completely coated, then leave to cool for 5 minutes.

03   Place a sheet of parchment paper on a sheet pan.

04   Butter your hands or spray with cooking oil, then divide the popcorn mixture into 8 portions and roll into balls (about ½ cup each). Transfer to the prepared sheet pan and leave to stand for 1–2 hours until set.

05   Store in an airtight container for up to 1 week.

Fudge, Cups, Truffles & Bites

TIP:

Try making these with flavored marshmallows or adding food coloring or chocolate to the mix!

HONEYCOMB

Makes 32 pieces

Homemade honeycomb is far easier to make than you may think, especially if you have a sugar thermometer. It's perfect for dipping into chocolate, decorating cakes or stirring into homemade ice cream. It's sweet, sugary, crunchy and packed with deep caramel and toffee flavors. What's not to love?

10 minutes
+ 1-2 hours setting

5 tbsp honey or
   corn syrup
1 cup (200g) superfine
   sugar
2 tsp baking soda

Fudge, Cups, Truffles & Bites

01   Line a 8 x 10in (20 x 25cm) baking pan with parchment paper (see page 16).

02   Put the honey or corn syrup and sugar into a large saucepan over a low heat and stir with a balloon whisk until the sugar dissolves (once it does, stop stirring or it will crystallize). Increase the heat to medium and leave the mixture to bubble for about 5 minutes until it turns deep amber in color and reaches 302°F (150°C) on a sugar thermometer. Be careful not to overcook the mixture because this can make the honeycomb fall flat.

03   Turn off the heat and quickly whisk in the baking soda until the mixture froths up and turns light and foamy. Be careful not to overmix, because this can also make the honeycomb fall flat.

04   Pour into your prepared pan, then leave to cool for a couple of hours until set. Remove from the pan and break into about 32 pieces. And there you have it: perfect honeycomb!

05   Make sure to store in an airtight container at room temperature for up to 5 days to ensure it stays nice and crunchy.

Serving suggestions 〰〰〰〰〰〰〰〰〰〰〰〰〰〰

The honeycomb pieces can be dipped into melted chocolate or bagged up as gifts.

TIP:

If sticky to touch once set, it likely didn't reach 302°F (150°C). If it's flat and very hard, it's likely overcooked or over-mixed.

CHOCOLATE HAZELNUT BROWNIE BITES

Makes 6

~~

These bites are soft, with crisp, chewy tops, and the best part is you probably already have all the ingredients in the house. They are best served slightly warm for a brownie-like texture. You can also top them with extra spread or even your favorite frosting.

20 minutes

½ cup (150g) chocolate-hazelnut spread (I use Nutella)
1 large egg
6 tbsp (50g) all-purpose flour

01   Preheat the oven to 350F°/180°C (160°C fan)/Gas mark 4 and line a 6-cup muffin pan with muffin liners.

02   Put the chocolate-hazelnut spread and egg into a large mixing bowl and mix together with a balloon whisk until smooth. Fold in the flour with a rubber spatula until just combined, then scoop the batter evenly into the muffin liners.

03   Bake for 15 minutes until the tops looks crispy and crackly. Leave to cool in the pan for 15 minutes, then transfer to a cooling rack to cool. Enjoy!

Fudge, Cups, Truffles & Bites

SPECULOOS CUPS

Makes 6

~~

If you love white chocolate and speculoos, these are the cups for you! They
have a white chocolate and speculoos shell, with a caramelized cookie and
cream cheese filling. They're sweet, cinnamony and definitely a crowd pleaser.

15 minutes
+ 1 hour 15 minutes
chilling

9oz (250g) white chocolate,
  broken into pieces
Scant ½ cup (130g)
  speculoos spread/cookie
  butter (I use Biscoff)
3.5oz (100g) speculoos
  cookies (I use Biscoff)
2oz (60g) full-fat
  cream cheese

01 Line a 6-cup muffin pan with cupcake liners.

02 Put the white chocolate and 100g (6 tbsp) of the speculoos
    spread (cookie butter) into a medium microwave-safe bowl
    and microwave on high in 30-second bursts, stirring at each
    interval, or melt using a double boiler (see page 17).

03 Scoop 1 tablespoon of the mixture into each cupcake liner
    and smooth out evenly, then pop them into the refrigerator
    for 15 minutes while you make the filling. Set aside the
    remaining melted chocolate mixture.

04 Put the cookies into a food processor and process until finely
    crushed. Alternatively, put them into a plastic bag and crush
    with a rolling pin. Tip into a medium bowl, then mix in the
    cream cheese and the remaining speculoos spread with
    a spoon until fully combined.

05 Remove the pan from the refrigerator, then scoop about
    1 tablespoon of the cookie mixture into each cupcake liner
    and press down firmly. Top with the remaining melted
    chocolate mixture and smooth it out to the edges, making
    sure the cookie mixture is completely covered.

06 Chill in the refrigerator for 1 hour, then remove from the
    liners and enjoy!

07 Store in an airtight container in the refrigerator for up to
    4 days.

TIP:
~~
You can easily
double this up to
make 12 cups instead
of 6 if you have
more mouths
to feed.

SALTED CARAMEL SAUCE

Makes about 1½ cups (350ml)

If you're as obsessed with salted caramel as I am, you need to have a good salted caramel sauce recipe on hand at all times. This one is sweet, salty and gooey, and perfect for drizzling over ice cream and brownies, or for using in drinks.

20 minutes
+ 20 minutes cooling

1 cup (200g) granulated sugar
6 tbsp (90g) salted butter, cut into pieces
⅔ cup (150ml) heavy cream
Pinch of sea salt

01 Put the sugar into a medium heavy saucepan and cook over a medium heat, stirring constantly with a balloon whisk, for about 10–15 minutes until melted and caramelized. It will first turn lumpy, then form bigger lumps, before it melts completely and turns a deep amber color. Be careful to watch the pan to avoid overcooking the sugar – it can burn quickly!

02 When the sugar has melted and bubbles form around the edge, carefully add the butter to the pan, taking care as the hot mixture may splutter. Stir constantly until the mixture is bubbling and well combined.

03 Slowly pour in the cream and add the salt, stirring gently until just combined. Turn off the heat and leave to cool in the pan for about 20 minutes, stirring a couple times while it's cooling.

04 Once cooled, give the sauce one final stir, then pour into a jar or airtight container. Store in the refrigerator for up to 2 weeks.

05 To serve, transfer to a microwave-safe bowl or jug and microwave on medium in 10-second intervals until it reaches your desired temperature, then drizzle it over your favorite desserts!

PEANUT BUTTER CHOCOLATE SHORTBREAD FINGERS

Makes 26

~

Buttery homemade shortbread and creamy peanut butter, covered in silky milk chocolate – it doesn't get much tastier than this! These bars are crunchy, soft and oh so chocolatey.

45 minutes
+ 1 hour cooling
and 1 hour setting

FOR THE SHORTBREAD

6oz (180g) unsalted butter, softened
Scant ½ cup (90g) granulated sugar
Scant 2 cups (250g) all-purpose flour

FOR THE TOPPING

7oz (200g) milk chocolate, broken into pieces
Heaping ½ cup (150g) creamy peanut butter

SWAP:
~

To make speculoos chocolate bars, swap the peanut butter for speculoos spread (cookie butter).

01 Preheat the oven to 350°F/180°C (160°C fan)/Gas mark 4 and line an 8in (20cm) square baking pan with parchment paper (see page 16).

02 To make the shortbread, put the butter, sugar and flour into a large mixing bowl and mix together with your fingertips until fully combined (it should look crumbly). Press the mixture into your prepared pan, making sure the top is level. Bake for 20–25 minutes until light golden brown, then leave to cool completely in the pan (about 1 hour).

03 When ready to coat, set a cooling rack over a sheet of parchment paper and melt the chocolate (see page 17).

04 Using a sharp knife, cut the shortbread into ½ x 4in (1.5 x 10cm) fingers, to make 26 pieces. Pop the peanut butter into a disposable piping bag and cut an opening at the tip about scant ½in (1cm) wide. Pipe over the top of the fingers. Smooth off the edges with the side of a knife or the back of a spoon.

05 Dip the bottom of the fingers into the melted chocolate, then transfer to the prepared cooling rack. Pour over the remaining chocolate, making sure the fingers are fully covered and letting any excess drip off. Leave to stand for 1 hour until set.

06 Store in an airtight container for up to 1 week.

55
~
Fudge, Cups, Truffles & Bites

CHOCOLATE PENGUIN BITES

Makes 10

~

These are so fun to make, especially with kids, and they're perfect for Christmas. There's no cooking involved, except for a bit of melting in the microwave, so they are really quick and easy to make. They make super-cute gifts and taste delicious. I mean, who doesn't love cream-filled chocolate sandwich cookies coated in chocolate?

20 minutes
+ 1 hour setting

10 cream-filled chocolate
   sandwich cookies
   (I use Oreos)
7oz (200g) milk chocolate
   or dark chocolate (at
   least 50% cocoa/cacao),
   broken into pieces and
   melted (see page 17)
10 small white chocolate
   buttons
20 edible candy eyeballs
10 orange candy-coated
   chocolate buttons (like
   M&Ms)

01 Set a cooling rack over a sheet of parchment paper or line a sheet pan with parchment paper.

02 Using 2 forks, coat each cookie in the melted chocolate, letting any excess drip off, then transfer to the prepared cooling rack or sheet pan.

03 While the chocolate on the cookies is still warm, gently place a white chocolate button on the center-bottom of each coated cookie (for the penguin's belly). Place 2 edible eyes above the white chocolate buttons on each, then place the orange candy-coated chocolate buttons in the middle of the eyes for the beak (see image). If the decorations move around on the coating too much, pop the cookies in the fridge for 1–2 minutes to slightly set the chocolate. You can also dab a small amount of melted chocolate on the back of the decorations to help them stick.

04 Chill in the refrigerator for 1 hour or leave to set at room temperature. Merry Christmas!

05 Store in an airtight container for up to 1 week.

CAKES, CUPCAKES and MUFFINS

~~

Chapter Two

If cakes are your thing, this chapter is for you...

I'm still absolutely mesmerized by the fact you can make a soft, moist, delicious cake with just a few ingredients!

You will find here my crazy popular 3-ingredient **Cookies and Cream Cake**, **Chocolate Hazelnut Doughnuts** and **Quick Scones**, plus my 4-ingredient **Flourless Chocolate Cake** and **Simple Sponge**.

These cakes are easily dressed up and can be topped with whatever you want. Go wild with different jams, frostings and spreads to suit your taste buds.

Just a pre-warning... you will never again have an excuse not to make a birthday cake!

So chocolatey!

COOKIES and CREAM CAKE

Serves 6-8

~~

This cake is one of my most popular recipes. Perfectly moist and chocolatey, it's absolutely delicious! You don't need any eggs or flour, and you don't even need an oven because this cake can be baked in the microwave in 7 minutes. You don't need to add a topping, but if you would like to decorate it, I would recommend a chocolate ganache (see below), which would work perfectly for a birthday cake.

20 minutes

30 cream-filled chocolate
   sandwich cookies
   (I use Oreos)
1 tsp baking powder
1¼ cups (270ml) whole or
   reduced fat milk, at room
   temperature

FOR THE GANACHE (OPTIONAL)
½ cup (125ml) heavy cream
5.25oz (150g) dark
   chocolate (at least 50%
   cocoa/cacao), broken
   into pieces

01 Spray a 7in (18cm) microwave-safe silicone cake mold with cooking oil and line the bottom with a circle of parchment paper (see page 16).

02 Separate the sandwich cookies and scrape the cream filling into a bowl, then set aside. Put the separated cookies into a food processor and process until finely crushed. Alternatively, put them into a plastic bag and crush with a rolling pin. Tip into a large mixing bowl, reserving about 1 tablespoon of the crumbs for the topping, if decorating the cake.

03 Add the baking powder to the large bowl of crumbs and mix together with a balloon whisk. Pour in the milk, then add the cookie cream filling to the bowl and mix together until smooth.

04 Pour into the prepared mold and microwave on high for 6–7 minutes until a toothpick inserted into the middle comes out clean. (If you prefer, you can bake the cake in an oven preheated to 350°F/180°C (160°C fan)/Gas mark 4 for 15 minutes.) Leave to cool in the mold, then invert the cake onto a cooling rack and peel off the lining paper.

05 The cake can be topped (see below for ganache) or cut into slices and served. Enjoy!

Optional ganache ~~~~~~~~~~~~~~~~

06 To make a chocolate ganache topping, heat the cream in a glass jug or microwave-safe bowl in the microwave for

about 1 minute until hot, but not boiling or bubbling – it may need longer depending on your microwave.

07 Put the chocolate into a medium heatproof bowl, then pour over the hot cream and gently stir until smooth and combined. Pour over the cooled cake, letting it drip over the edges, then sprinkle with the reserved cookie crumbs.

08 Store in an airtight container in the refrigerator for up to 3 days.

CHOCOLATE COOKIE CAKE

Makes 9 squares

No flour or eggs needed for this cake! It's super soft and moist, and really quick and easy to make. Top it with your favorite icing or spread and no one will ever know you made it with just cookies, baking powder and milk.

20 minutes

12.4oz (350g) chocolate-covered digestive biscuits
2 tsp baking powder
1½ cups (350ml) whole milk, at room temperature

01 Preheat the oven to 350°F/180°C (160°C fan)/Gas mark 4 and line an 8in (20cm) square baking pan with parchment paper (see page 16).

02 Put the biscuits into a food processor and process until finely crushed. Alternatively, put them into a plastic bag and crush with a rolling pin. Tip into a large mixing bowl, then mix in the baking powder with a balloon whisk until combined.

03 Pour in the milk and gently fold in with a rubber spatula until fully combined. The batter should still look slightly lumpy. Pour into your prepared pan and smooth it out to the edges.

04 Bake for 15 minutes until a toothpick inserted into the center comes out with just a few crumbs on it. If you overbake it, the cake can turn out too dry. Leave to cool in the pan for 10 minutes, then transfer to a serving plate or cooling rack. Once cool, cut into 9 squares and serve.

05 Store in an airtight container for up to 3–4 days.

TIP:

To make this cake extra chocolatey, add 1 tbsp cocoa powder or 7 tbsp (100g) chocolate chips to the batter.

Optional topping

To give this cake an extra boost of flavor, I would recommend topping it with your favorite chocolate buttercream, chocolate ganache (see pages 62–63) or melted chocolate-hazelnut spread.

PINEAPPLE CAKE

Serves 8

This cake is moist, sweet and fruity. It takes just a few minutes to whip up, then you can relax while it bakes. It's perfect for all occasions, especially the summer months when you can get outside and enjoy it in the garden. You can also decorate it however you wish to suit your taste buds.

1 hour

Scant 2 cups (250g)
   self-raising flour
1 cup (200g) superfine
   sugar
Scant 2 cups (450g)
   canned crushed
   pineapple with juice

01 Preheat the oven to 350°F/180°C (160°C fan)/Gas mark 4. Spray an 8in (20cm) round springform cake pan with cooking oil and line the bottom with a circle of parchment paper (see page 16).

02 Put all the ingredients into a large mixing bowl and mix together with a wooden spoon or rubber spatula. Pour into your prepared pan and smooth out evenly.

03 Bake for 50–60 minutes until a toothpick inserted into the middle comes out clean. Leave to cool in the pan for 10 minutes, then transfer to a cooling rack to cool or serve the cake while it's still fresh and warm.

04 Store in an airtight container for up to 3 days.

Optional topping

Top the cake with Cream Cheese Frosting (see page 225), like in the photo, or serve with your favorite ice cream or whipped cream. Delicious!

SPECULOOS CAKE

Serves 8
~~

This cake is a must for speculoos cookie lovers. It's soft, moist and so easy
to make. With speculoos spread (cookie butter) as the main ingredient,
this cake is packed with sweet, cinnamon flavors.

**40 minutes
+ 40 minutes cooling**

2¼ cups (525g) speculoos
  spread/cookie butter
  (I use Biscoff)
1½ tsp baking powder
2 large eggs

FOR THE TOPPING (OPTIONAL)
2 speculoos cookies (I use
  Biscoff), finely crushed

01 Preheat the oven to 350°F/180°C (160°C fan)/Gas mark 4
    and line the bottom of an 8in (20cm) round springform cake
    pan with a circle of parchment paper (see page 16).

02 Put 1⅔ cups (400g) of the speculoos spread (cookie butter)
    into a microwave-safe bowl and microwave on high in
    30-second bursts, stirring at each interval, until runny and
    smooth. Leave it to cool for about 5 minutes.

03 Transfer to a large mixing bowl, then stir in the baking
    powder with a balloon whisk. Gradually mix in the eggs
    until fully combined, then pour into your prepared pan and
    smooth out evenly with the back of a spoon.

04 Bake for 30 minutes, or until a toothpick inserted into
    the middle comes out clean. Leave to cool in the pan for
    30 minutes, then transfer to a cooling rack.

05 Melt the remaining speculoos spread in a microwave-safe
    bowl as above, then pour over the cake, spreading it out
    with the back of a spoon and letting it drip over the edge.

06 Store in an airtight container for 4–5 days.

Optional topping ~~~~~~~~~~~~~~~~~~~~~~~~~~~

At Step 5, sprinkle the crushed cookies over the top to decorate,
if desired.

STUFFED CHOCOLATE MUFFINS

Makes 12

These taste just like the Brownie Bites on page 48, but even better, as they're stuffed with a cream-filled chocolate sandwich cookie. They're soft and chewy, with a crispy top, and they're packed with chocolate-hazelnut flavors. Absolutely delicious!

40 minutes

2 large eggs

1 cup (300g) chocolate-hazelnut spread (I use Nutella)

12 cream-filled chocolate sandwich cookies (I use Oreos)

01 Preheat the oven to 400°F/200°C (180°C fan)/Gas mark 6 and line a 12-cup muffin pan with cupcake liners.

02 In a medium mixing bowl, beat the eggs with an electric hand mixer until light and frothy, then mix in the chocolate-hazelnut spread until fully combined.

03 Scoop 1 tablespoon of the mixture into each liner, then press a cookie into each one. Add another 1½–2 tablespoons of the batter on top of each, making sure the cookies are fully covered. The liners should be about two thirds full.

04 Bake in the oven for 20–25 minutes until the top and edges look nice and crisp.

05 Leave to cool in the pan for 20 minutes, then transfer to a cooling rack to cool completely.

06 Store in an airtight container for up to 5 days.

Serving suggestion

You can also serve the cups warm with a scoop of ice cream and chocolate sauce. Yum!

SWAP:

Use chocolate truffles instead of cream-filled chocolate sandwich cookies for a melting middle!

BANANA MUFFINS

Makes 12

~~

If you love banana bread but don't always have time to make it, these easy banana muffins will be your new go-to recipe. They're super soft and moist, and packed with banana flavor. We're kind of cheating here as these are made with a cake box mix, but no one will know, I promise! They take less than 5 minutes to make and just 20 minutes in the oven before they're ready to eat.

25 minutes

3 large overripe bananas
1 x 15oz (425g) box vanilla cake mix
2 large eggs

01 Preheat the oven to 350°F/180°C (160°C fan)/Gas mark 4 and line a 12-cup muffin pan with muffin liners.

02 Put the bananas into a large mixing bowl and mash together with the back of a fork until smooth. Pour in the cake mix and add the eggs, then gently mix together with a balloon whisk until just combined. Scoop the batter into your muffin liners.

03 Bake for 15–20 minutes until a toothpick inserted into the center of a muffin comes out clean. Transfer to a cooling rack and leave to cool. Enjoy!

04 Store in an airtight container at room temperature for up to 4 days.

Cakes, Cupcakes & Muffins

TIP:
~~
If you want to add in extras like chocolate chips, fold them into the batter in step 2.

SWAP:
~~
Replace the vanilla cake mix with chocolate mix to make chocolate banana muffins.

CHOCOLATE HAZELNUT DOUGHNUTS

Makes 6

If you thought doughnuts were difficult to make, think again! These are soft, chocolatey and really easy. Topped with chocolate-hazelnut spread, they make a delicious snack with a cup of tea or coffee. I recommend using a silicone doughnut mold for this recipe.

20 minutes + 1 hour cooling

⅔ cup (185g) chocolate-hazelnut spread (I use Nutella) + scant ¼ cup (70g) for the topping
2 large eggs
⅔ cup (90g) all-purpose flour

01 Preheat the oven to 340°F/170°C (150°C fan)/Gas mark 3½ and spray a doughnut mold with cooking oil. I recommend using a silicone doughnut mold with 3in (7.5cm) diameter doughnut shapes.

02 Put the ⅔ cup (185g) chocolate-hazelnut spread into a large mixing bowl. Add the eggs and flour and mix together with a balloon whisk until fully combined.

03 Transfer the batter to a disposable piping bag and cut off the tip, then pipe into your prepared doughnut mold, filling each hole about three quarters full.

04 Bake in the oven for 10–12 minutes until a toothpick inserted into a doughnut comes out clean. Leave to cool in the mold for 20 minutes, then transfer to a cooling rack to cool completely.

05 Once cool, put the remaining chocolate-hazelnut spread into a microwave-safe bowl and microwave on high in 20-second bursts, stirring at each interval, until runny and smooth. Dip the top of each doughnut into the melted spread, or drizzle it over the tops. Enjoy!

TIP:

Add sprinkles or chopped hazelnuts for decoration and extra flavor.

QUICK SCONES

Makes about 12

These quick scones are so delicious and incredibly easy to make. They're light and fluffy, with crisp, golden tops and oh so buttery – perfect for any garden party, afternoon tea or picnic. Serve them with cream and jam, or why not make them savory with cheese and chutney, or other toppings of your choice?

30 minutes

2¾ cups + 2 tbsp (375g)
   self-raising flour + extra
   for dusting
5 tbsp (75g) unsalted
   butter, cubed
1 cup (250ml) whole milk
   + extra if needed

01 Preheat the oven to 400°F/200°C (180°C fan)/Gas mark 6 and line a large sheet pan with parchment paper.

02 Put the flour and butter into a large mixing bowl and rub together with your fingertips until the mixture is crumbly. Make a well in the middle, then pour in the milk and mix together with your hands to form a soft dough, adding more milk if the dough is too dry.

03 Flour a clean, flat surface and your hands, then tip the dough onto the surface and knead until smooth. Press the dough down with your hands or a floured rolling pin until about ¾in (2cm) thick, then cut out circles using a 2.5in (6.5cm) round cookie cutter or the rim of a glass. Re-roll the excess dough, then repeat until you have about 12 scones.

04 Bake in the oven for 15–20 minutes until risen and the tops are golden. Serve warm.

05 Store in an airtight container at room temperature for up to 3 days.

Cakes, Cupcakes & Muffins

FLOURLESS CHOCOLATE CAKE

Serves 10

~

This cake is rich and silky, the ultimate dessert for chocolate lovers. It almost has a chocolate torte/mousse-like texture. It looks and tastes just like a chocolate cake at an expensive restaurant, so no one will guess it's made with only 4 ingredients!

50 minutes + overnight chilling

8oz (225g) unsalted butter, cut into pieces
1lb (500g) dark chocolate (about 50% cocoa/cacao), broken into pieces
7 large eggs
½ cup (100g) granulated sugar (optional)

01 Preheat the oven to 340°F/170°C (150°C fan)/Gas mark 3½ and grease an 8in (20cm) round springform cake pan with butter. Line the bottom of the pan with a circle of parchment paper (see page 16), then wrap foil underneath and up the outside of the pan. Place into a larger, round cake pan or a large, deep baking pan (this will be the water bath for the cake, which helps it to cook through more evenly).

02 Put the butter and chocolate into a medium microwave-safe bowl and microwave on high in 30-second bursts, stirring at each interval, until runny and smooth. Leave to cool almost completely.

03 Put the eggs and sugar into a large mixing bowl and beat together with an electric hand mixer for about 10 minutes until tripled in volume. Fold in half the cooled chocolate with a rubber spatula, then pour in the remaining chocolate and stir gently until fully combined.

04 Pour the cake batter into your prepared lined pan, then carefully fill the outer pan halfway up the sides with boiling water. Carefully transfer to the oven and bake for 30–35 minutes until the edges are firm and the top is crisp and glazed. An instant-read thermometer inserted into the middle should read 140°F (60°C).

05 Remove the cake from the water bath and leave to cool completely in the pan, then cover with plastic wrap and chill in the refrigerator overnight. When ready to serve, remove from the pan, loosening the edges if needed. Enjoy!

06 Store in the refrigerator for up to 4 days.

TIP:

~

Dust the cake with powdered sugar and serve with cream and berries, if desired.

SIMPLE SPONGE

Serves 10

~~

This sponge cake is one of the easiest cakes you can make. It's light, fluffy and so tasty. With only 4 main ingredients, it is also inexpensive and incredibly versatile – feel free to fill and decorate it as you wish (I've made a few suggestions below, but the options are endless). Perfect for all occasions!

50 minutes
+ 1 hour cooling

8oz (225g) unsalted margarine or butter, softened

Generous 1 cup (225g) superfine sugar

4 large eggs

1¾ cups (225g) self-raising flour

01   Preheat the oven to 340°F/170°C (150°C fan)/Gas mark 3½. Grease 2 x 8in (20cm) round springform cake pans with butter and line the bottoms with circles of parchment paper (see page 16).

02   Put the margarine or butter and sugar into a large mixing bowl and beat with an electric hand mixer until light and fluffy. Add the eggs, one at a time, until just incorporated. Sift in the flour, then fold it in with a rubber spatula until just combined. If the batter is too dry, add 1–2 tablespoons of milk.

03   Divide the batter between your prepared cake pans and smooth out evenly with the back of a spoon.

04   Bake in the oven for 30–40 minutes until golden brown and a toothpick inserted into the middle of the cakes comes out clean. Leave to cool in the pans for 30 minutes, then transfer to a cooling rack to cool completely.

05   Now this is the fun part! Once cooled, remove the cakes from the pans and peel off the lining paper. Place one of the sponges onto a serving plate and spread over your filling of choice. Top with the second cake and decorate as desired. (See serving suggestions below.)

06   Store in an airtight container for 3–4 days.

Serving suggestions ~~~~~~~~~~~~~~~~~~~~~~~~~~~~~

The classic filling is buttercream and strawberry or raspberry jam, dusted with powdered or superfine sugar, but you could also try lemon curd, fresh whipped cream and seasonal berries, or even chocolate spread.

PECAN BUNS

Makes 6

~

If you love sweet and sticky pastries, you will love this simple version of pecan buns. They are made with crescent roll dough, meaning they're incredibly buttery and flaky. The sweet caramel glaze covers the pecans and seeps into the dough, creating the most amazingly delicious mini buns.

30 minutes

1 x 8oz tube crescent
   roll dough
6 tbsp light brown sugar
4 tbsp (60g) salted or
   unsalted butter, cut into 2
   tsp (10g) pieces
6 tbsp roughly chopped
   pecans

01 Preheat the oven to 400°F/200°C (180°C fan)/Gas mark 6 and grease a 6-cup muffin pan with butter.

02 Unroll the dough onto a clean, flat surface and cut along the perforated lines to get 6 pieces. Following the package directions, roll the dough pieces from the shortest edge to the tip to form croissant shapes. Cut each rolled piece of dough in half and set aside.

03 Put 1 tablespoon of the sugar, 1 tablespoon water, 2 tsp (10g) of the butter and 1 tablespoon of the pecans into each of the muffin cups, then press 2 of the dough halves on top in each hole (you will need to bend the dough to fit).

04 Bake for 15–20 minutes until the tops are crisp and golden brown and the pastries are cooked through. Leave to cool for 5 minutes, then remove from the pan.

05 Turn the pastries upside down (pecans facing upwards) to serve. These are best eaten on the day of baking. Enjoy!

TIP:

~

If you don't want to add the pecans, you can omit them or use a different type of nut.

MUG CAKES

~

Chapter Three

Make in minutes

There's something about a mug cake that's so comforting. I think it's the fact you can make it in minutes, then sit on the sofa and devour it with a spoon. In this chapter, you will find chocolatey mug cakes, one packed with peanut butter, a warming apple crumble (made in ramekins, not mugs, but close enough) and even a cinnamon roll made in a mug. If you've had mug cake disasters before, don't worry – we've all been there! Here are some tips:

- **Use a large mug** so your batter has enough room to rise without spilling over. Alternatively, all mug cakes that serve 1 can be made into 2 smaller cakes. Just divide the batter between 2 mugs and place both in the microwave. Check them halfway through the stated cooking time. If they're not ready, continue cooking in 10–20 second intervals until they're done.

- **Check your microwave wattage.** The cooking times in this book are based on a 700W microwave. If your microwave is more powerful, turn it down to a medium or medium-high setting and check the cake halfway through cooking.

- **Heat-treat your flour** and let it cool before making any mug cake that uses flour. See page 17 for instructions on this.

- **Don't overmix your batter** – overmixing batter can lead to tough, rubbery cakes, and no one wants that! Overcooking can be another reason for this.

- **If you want your mug cake to look pretty**, transfer it to another mug after baking, or just dress it up with a little whipped cream, chocolate spread or fruit and powdered sugar.

Hug in a mug

CHOCOLATE HAZELNUT MUG CAKE

Serves 1

If you thought mug cakes were boring and dry, think again! This mug cake is easy to make and it's ultra-moist. You don't need any flour, which also means it's gluten-free. It's super chocolatey and perfect if you love chocolate-hazelnut spread. Just mix all the ingredients together and pop in the microwave – it really is as easy as that.

5 minutes

1 large egg
6½ tbsp (120g) chocolate-
   hazelnut spread
   (I use Nutella)
2 tsp 100% cocoa powder

01   Put all the ingredients into a large mug and mix together with a fork until fully combined. The batter should be thick and smooth.

02   Microwave on high for 1 minute 10 seconds until no wet batter remains around the edge of the cake. A little remaining wet batter at the base of the mug is totally fine.

03   Leave to cool for 2 minutes before digging in!

Serving suggestions

Top your mug cake with an extra blob of chocolate-hazelnut spread or maybe even some whipped cream for extra deliciousness.

TIP:

Add extras to the batter, such as cookies, candy-coated chocolate buttons or chocolate chips.

SEE THIS PICTURED ON THE NEXT PAGE

SPECULOOS MUG CAKE

Serves 1

~

If you love speculoos spread (cookie butter), this is the mug cake for you. You can whip up your own individual cake in just minutes and enjoy eating it straight out of the mug with a spoon. It's super soft and fluffy, and packed with delicious caramelized cookie and cinnamon flavors – so good, and perfect for movie night!

5 minutes

- 4 tbsp (60g) speculoos spread/cookie butter (I use Biscoff)
- 4 tbsp (60ml) milk
- 4 tbsp (35g) all-purpose flour, heat-treated (see page 17)
- ¼ tsp baking powder

01   Put all the ingredients into a large mug and mix together with a fork until fully combined. The batter should be thick and smooth.

02   Microwave on high for 1 minute 20 seconds until a toothpick inserted into the middle comes out with just a few crumbs and there is no wet batter remaining. The top of the cake should spring back when lightly pressed.

03   Leave to cool for 2 minutes before devouring!

TIP:
~

Top with a thin layer of speculoos spread (cookie butter) and let it melt for extra speculoos flavor!

SEE THIS PICTURED ON THE NEXT PAGE

Chocolate Hazelnut
Mug Cake

Speculoos
Mug Cake

Peanut Butter Mug Cake

Banana Bread Mug Cake

BANANA BREAD MUG CAKE

Serves 1

There's nothing like a warm, gooey banana cake... especially when you can make it in about 5 minutes in a mug! It's moist, packed with flavor and absolutely delicious. Jazz it up by adding your favorite fillings and toppings.

5 minutes

½ large overripe banana
3½ tbsp (30g) all-purpose
  flour, heat-treated
  (see page 17)
¼ tsp baking powder
1 tbsp maple syrup
  or honey
2 tsp milk

01 Put the banana into a bowl and mash it with the back of a fork until it forms a purée.

02 Transfer to a large mug, then add the remaining ingredients and mix together until fully combined.

03 Microwave on high for 1 minute until no wet batter remains and a toothpick inserted into the center comes out with just a few crumbs.

04 Leave to cool for about 2 minutes before eating. Enjoy!

Optional extra

For a melting middle, add half the batter, a scoop of peanut butter or chocolate spread, and top with the remaining batter!

TIP:
Try adding 1 tbsp of milk chocolate chips when you add all the ingredients in Step 2.

TIP:
You could also add nuts or a pinch of ground cinnamon to the batter for extra flavor.

SEE THIS PICTURED ON THE PREVIOUS PAGE

PEANUT BUTTER MUG CAKE

Serves 1

A warm gooey, peanut butter mug cake is just perfect for an evening in. It takes no more than 5 minutes before it's ready to eat and is incredibly versatile – you can add all your favorite fillings and toppings. If peanut butter is your thing, this is the cake for you!

5 minutes

2 tbsp (35g) creamy smooth peanut butter

3½ tbsp (30g) all-purpose flour, heat-treated (see page 17)

¼ tsp baking powder

3 tbsp (40g) granulated sugar

3 tbsp (45ml) skim milk

01 Put all the ingredients into a large mug and mix together with a fork until fully combined. The batter should be thick and smooth.

02 Microwave on high for 1 minute 15 seconds until no wet batter remains around the edge of the cake. If there's still wet batter remaining, heat for another 10 seconds.

03 Leave to cool for 2 minutes, then indulge!

Serving suggestions

Top your mug cake with extra peanut butter or whipped cream to dress it up.

93

Mug Cakes

TIP:

Try adding 1 tbsp of milk chocolate chips when you add all the ingredients in Step 1.

SEE THIS PICTURED ON THE PREVIOUS PAGE

CINNAMON ROLL
in a mug

Serves 1

If you love cinnamon rolls as much as I do, but don't like how long they take to make, you will adore this recipe! It's soft, it's doughy and it takes less than 10 minutes. With a buttery, cinnamon filling and a sweet glaze, this is everything you could want from a cinnamon roll, without all the fuss. There are a little over 5 ingredients if you make the optional glaze, but I really recommend that you do.

10 minutes

3½ tbsp (60g) Greek yogurt (any fat percentage)
6 tbsp (50g) self-raising flour, heat-treated (see page 17) + extra if needed and for dusting

FOR THE FILLING
2 tsp (10g) unsalted butter, melted
1 tbsp granulated sugar
½ tsp ground cinnamon

FOR THE GLAZE (OPTIONAL)
3 tbsp powdered sugar
2 tsp milk

01 Grease a small/medium mug with butter or spray with cooking oil.

02 Put the yogurt and flour into a small bowl and mix together until they come together to form a dough. Knead with your hands until it is no longer sticky, adding more flour after a couple of minutes if needed.

03 Transfer the dough to a floured surface and roll out to a rectangle measuring about 10 x 6in (25 x 15cm).

04 In a small bowl, mix together the filling ingredients until fully combined, then spread over the dough, leaving a border of about a scant ½in (1cm) around the edges. Fold in the long edges (to stop any of the filling from seeping out during cooking), then loosely roll up the dough from one of the short edges.

05 Pop the roll into the prepared mug and microwave on high for 50–60 seconds until the dough is piping hot. Try to avoid overcooking, as the dough will become chewy.

Optional glaze ~~~~~~~~~~~~~~~~~~~~~~~~~

In a small bowl or another mug, mix together the powdered sugar and milk with a spoon until smooth. Pour the glaze over the warm roll, and there you have it. You could also turn the roll out onto a plate to eat with a knife and fork, if you prefer.

CHOCOLATE HAZELNUT ROLL
in a mug

Serves 1
~~

A warm, doughy roll stuffed with melted chocolate-hazelnut spread and topped with a sweet chocolate glaze – mug cakes don't get much better than this! You only need two ingredients to make the dough, then slather on the spread for the ultimate dessert.

10 minutes

3½ tbsp (60g) Greek yogurt (any fat percentage)

6 tbsp (50g) self-raising flour, heat-treated (see page 17) + extra if needed and for dusting

Chocolate-hazelnut spread (I use Nutella), for the filling (as much or as little as you like)

FOR THE GLAZE

3 tbsp powdered sugar

2 tsp milk

1 tsp chocolate-hazelnut spread, melted

01 Grease a small/medium mug with butter or spray with cooking oil.

02 Put the yogurt and flour into a small bowl and mix until they come together to form a dough. Knead with your hands until it is no longer sticky, adding more flour after a couple of minutes if needed.

03 Transfer the dough to a floured surface and roll out to a rectangle measuring about 10 x 6in (25 x 15cm). Spread chocolate-hazelnut spread over the dough, leaving a border of about a scant ½in (1cm) around the edges. Fold in the long edges (to stop any melted spread from seeping out during cooking), then loosely roll up the dough from one of the short edges.

04 Pop the roll into the prepared mug and microwave on high for 1 minute until the dough is piping hot. Try to avoid overcooking, as the dough will become chewy and tough.

05 Meanwhile, in a small bowl or another mug, make the glaze. Mix together the powdered sugar and milk with a spoon until smooth, then add the melted chocolate-hazelnut spread and mix until combined.

06 Pour the glaze over the warm roll in the mug and dig in! You could also turn the roll out onto a plate to eat with a knife and fork, if you prefer.

SWAP:
~~

You could easily swap the chocolate-hazelnut spread for speculoos spread (cookie butter).

Mug Cakes
~~

APPLE CRUMBLE MUG CAKE

Serves 2

~

There's nothing like a warm apple crumble on a cold winter's day, and when you don't want to make a whole dish, this recipe is exactly what you need. Unlike the other recipes in this chapter, it's baked in the oven, but it's as comforting as any mug cake, plus quick and easy to make. And you only need 5 ingredients, so let's go!

35 minutes

FOR THE FILLING

1 tbsp (15g) granulated
  sugar
¼ tsp ground cinnamon
1 large apple, peeled,
  cored and cubed

FOR THE TOPPING

4¾ tbsp (40g) all-purpose
  flour
3 tbsp (40g) granulated
  sugar
3 tbsp (40g) unsalted
  butter, cold and cubed

01 Preheat the oven to 350°F/180°C (160°C fan)/Gas mark 4.

02 Mix together the sugar and cinnamon in a small bowl or mug until combined, then add the chopped apple and toss until coated in the mixture.

03 In another small bowl or mug, mix together the flour, sugar and cold butter until combined. I prefer to do this with my fingertips until it becomes crumbly.

04 Scoop the apple mixture into 2 separate ramekins, then evenly crumble over the topping.

05 Bake for 25 minutes until the tops are golden brown and the apples are soft.

Serving suggestion ~~~~~~~~~~~~~~~~

Serve warm with cream or ice cream. Yum!

TIP:

~

Add cinnamon
and oats to the
topping for even
more flavor!

TRAY BAKES

~

Chapter Four

I just LOVE a good tray bake

This may be my favorite chapter in the book... I just love a good tray bake. Whether it's a super-fudgy chocolate brownie or a soft, gooey flapjack, they are perfect for sharing and generally pretty easy to transport as well, making them great for parties and special occasions.

In this chapter, you will find **Crispy Marshmallow Bars**, **Speculoos Rocky Road**, **Tangy Lemon Bars** and lots more!

Feel free to mix and match and swap out ingredients to make these recipes your own. I mean, you can't really go wrong with adding a few extras to a rocky road.

Have fun!

Traybake heaven

CARAMEL SHORTBREAD ROCKY ROAD

Makes 16 pieces

~~

Caramel shortbread, marshmallows and chocolate – what a combo!
This rocky road is super chocolatey with so many textures: it's crunchy, creamy,
soft and chewy, and is so easy to make, with no baking involved.

15 minutes + 3 hours chilling

11oz (320g) caramel
shortbread chocolate
bars (I use Twix), cut into
scant ½in (1cm) pieces

1½ cups (70g) mini
marshmallows

18.5oz (525g) milk
chocolate, broken
into pieces and melted
(see page 17)

01 Line an 8in (20cm) square baking pan with parchment
paper (see page 16).

02 Put 9oz (260g) of the caramel shortbread pieces and the
mini marshmallows into a mixing bowl and stir together.

03 Leave the melted milk chocolate to cool for 5 minutes (to
help prevent the chocolate on the caramel shortbread from
melting), then pour it over the marshmallow mixture and stir
until everything is completely coated.

04 Scoop the mixture into your prepared pan, pressing it out
to the edges. Press the remaining 2oz (60g) of caramel
shortbread pieces on top.

05 Chill in the refrigerator for 3 hours, or until the chocolate
has set, then using a sharp, warm knife (see page 11), cut
into 16 pieces. Enjoy!

06 Store in an airtight container in the refrigerator or at room
temperature for up to 4 days.

SWAP:

~~

Swap the
chocolate bars for
another type of bar
or cookie, for a
totally different
rocky road!

CHOCOLATE HAZELNUT BROWNIES

Makes 16

These brownies are so fudgy and chocolatey, with a crisp, crackly top.
They're everything you could want from a brownie, but are made with
just 3 ingredients – amazing!

30 minutes
+ overnight chilling
(optional)

1¼ cups (370g) chocolate-
  hazelnut spread
  (I use Nutella)
2 large eggs
½ cup (65g) all-purpose
  flour

01 Preheat the oven to 350°F/180°C (160°C fan)/Gas mark 4
   and line an 8in (20cm) square baking pan with parchment
   paper (see page 16).

02 Put the chocolate-hazelnut spread and eggs into a large
   mixing bowl and beat together with an electric hand mixer
   until fully combined. Add the flour and fold in with a wooden
   spoon or rubber spatula.

03 Scoop the batter into your prepared baking pan and spread
   it out evenly with the back of a spoon.

04 Bake for 20 minutes until a light, crackly crust forms.
   Leave to cool completely in the pan for 2–3 hours or
   chill in the refrigerator overnight for extra fudgy and
   delicious brownies. Cut into 16 squares, serve and enjoy!

05 Store in an airtight container in the refrigerator or at room
   temperature for up to 5 days.

TIP:
Try adding
chocolate chips,
candy-coated
chocolate buttons
or nuts for extra
flavor.

TIP:
You could add
a layer of cream-filled
chocolate
sandwich
cookies through the
middle to make
cookie brownies!

COOKIES and CREAM MARSHMALLOW BARS

Makes 16

~~

These marshmallow bars are sweet, gooey and packed with cream-filled chocolate sandwich cookies! Cut them into bars, then store them in the refrigerator for a quick snack, or why not wrap them up and give them as a gift or take them on a picnic?

**15 minutes
+ 1–2 hours chilling**

56 cream-filled chocolate
   sandwich cookies
   (I use Oreos)
2 tbsp (30g) unsalted
   butter
4 cups (200g) mini
   marshmallows

01   Line an 8in (20cm) square baking pan with parchment paper (see page 16).

02   Break the cookies into quarters using your hands or a knife and chopping board, then set aside.

03   Put the butter and mini marshmallows into a large saucepan and warm over a medium heat, stirring constantly with a wooden spoon, until completely melted and combined. Remove from the heat, then add your crushed cookies, folding them in until they are completely coated.

04   Scoop the mixture into your prepared pan and press down firmly. If it's very sticky, use a wet glass to press it down.

05   Chill in the refrigerator for 1–2 hours until set, then cut into 16 bars and enjoy!

06   Store in an airtight container in the refrigerator for up to 4 days.

CRISPY MARSHMALLOW BARS

Makes 16

~

I had to include an ultra-easy marshmallow bar recipe in this book. They're so delicious and so versatile – you can pretty much use any crispy cereal you want, and add extras to change the flavor or to suit the occasion. Think mini cookie cereal with added chocolate chips, or chocolate puffed rice and candy-coated chocolate buttons – so good!

15 minutes
+ 1-2 hours chilling

7 tbsp (100g) unsalted butter
7 cups (350g) mini marshmallows
6½ cups (170g) puffed rice cereal (I use Rice Krispies)

01   Line an 8in (20cm) square baking pan with parchment paper (see page 16).

02   Put the butter and mini marshmallows into a large saucepan and warm over a medium heat, stirring constantly with a wooden spoon, until completely melted and combined. Remove from the heat, then add your puffed rice, folding it in until completely coated.

03   Scoop the mixture into your prepared pan and press down firmly. If it's very sticky, use a wet glass to press it down.

04   Chill in the refrigerator for 1–2 hours until set, then cut into 16 bars, serve and enjoy!

05   Store in an airtight container at room temperature (not in the refrigerator) for up to 4 days.

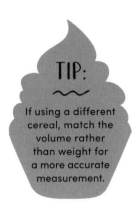

TIP:

~

If using a different cereal, match the volume rather than weight for a more accurate measurement.

PEANUT BUTTER CORNFLAKE BARS

Makes 16

~

These bars are crazy delicious! They're nutty, sweet and crunchy, and are perfect as a quick snack at home or on the go. They take 10 minutes to make, then just let them set in the refrigerator and they're ready to eat.

10 minutes
+ 1-2 hours chilling

¾ cup (240g) + 2 tbsp)
  creamy peanut butter
1 cup (250ml) honey
4 cups (110g) cornflakes

01 Line an 8in (20cm) square baking pan with parchment paper (see page 16).

02 Put the peanut butter and honey into a large saucepan and warm over a medium heat, stirring constantly with a wooden spoon, until completely melted and combined. Remove from the heat, then add your cornflakes, folding them in until they are completely coated.

03 Scoop the mixture into your prepared pan and press down firmly. Chill in the refrigerator for 1–2 hours until set, then cut into 16 bars and enjoy!

04 Store in an airtight container in the refrigerator for up to 3 days.

SWAP:
~

For a different but equally delicious bar, use speculoos spread (cookie butter) instead of peanut butter.

RASPBERRY CRUMBLE BARS

Makes 16

~

These bars just melt in your mouth! They have a shortbread base and a raspberry jam filling, topped with a crisp, buttery crumble. They're perfect for summer or winter and you can switch up the jam for a totally new flavor every time you make them.

1 hour 10 minutes

2¼ cups (290g)
  all-purpose flour
Generous ¾ cup (160g)
  granulated sugar
7oz (200g) cold unsalted
  butter, cubed
⅔ cup (200g) raspberry
  jam

01 Preheat the oven to 350°F/180°C (160°C fan)/Gas mark 4 and line an 8in (20cm) square baking pan with parchment paper (see page 16).

02 Put the flour and sugar into a large mixing bowl, then add the butter and rub it in with your fingertips until it looks like breadcrumbs. Spoon two thirds of the mixture into your prepared pan and press down firmly with your hands or the back of a spoon. Pop the remaining mixture into the refrigerator.

03 Spread the jam over the shortbread base, spreading it to the edges. Remove the bowl from the refrigerator and crumble over the reserved mixture, making sure the jam is fully covered.

04 Bake for 50–60 minutes until the top is crisp, golden brown and cooked through. Leave to cool completely in the pan, then cut into 16 squares and serve.

05 Store in an airtight container at room temperature (not in the refrigerator) for up to 5 days.

SWAP:
~
Use the jam of your choice. You could also use lemon curd or chocolate spread for a totally different taste.

CHOCOLATE MALT BALL ROCKY ROAD

Makes 16

〜

This rocky road is so chunky and satisfyingly crunchy. It's loaded with chocolate malt balls, mini marshmallows and chocolate-hazelnut spread, which keeps the bake slightly soft and creamy, even after being in the refrigerator, making it easier to bite and to cut – result!

15 minutes + 3 hours chilling

9oz (250g) chocolate malt balls

1½ cups (70g) mini marshmallows

14oz (400g) milk chocolate, broken into pieces

5½ tbsp (100g) chocolate-hazelnut spread

01 Line an 8in (20cm) square baking pan with parchment paper (see page 16).

02 Mix together the chocolate malt balls and mini marshmallows in a mixing bowl. Set aside.

03 Put the milk chocolate and chocolate spread into a medium microwave-safe bowl and microwave on high in 30-second bursts, stirring at each interval, until melted. Alternatively, melt in a double boiler (see page 17).

04 Leave the melted chocolate mixture to cool for 5 minutes (to help prevent the chocolate covering on the malt balls from melting), then pour it over the marshmallow mixture and stir until everything is completely coated.

05 Scoop the mixture into your prepared pan, pressing it out to the edges, then chill in the refrigerator for 3 hours, or until the chocolate has set. Using a sharp knife, cut into 16 pieces and enjoy!

06 Store in an airtight container in the refrigerator or at room temperature for up to 4 days.

SWAP:
〜

Replace the milk chocolate with white for a super sweet and creamy alternative.

Tray Bakes

SPECULOOS ROCKY ROAD

Makes 16

~~~

If you are in need of a really quick and easy bake, with no actual baking involved, this is the recipe for you. It's also great for getting the kids involved, and I mean, who doesn't love speculoos, white chocolate and marshmallows? Have fun!

15 minutes + 1 hour chilling

9oz (250g) speculoos cookies (I use Biscoff) + extra to decorate (optional)

1 cup (50g) mini marshmallows

18 oz (510g) white chocolate, broken into pieces

6 tbsp (90g) speculoos spread/cookie butter (I use Biscoff)

01 Line an 8in (20cm) square baking pan with parchment paper (see page 16).

02 Put the cookies into a bowl and break them up roughly with your hands, or use a knife and chopping board. Tip into a large heatproof mixing bowl and stir in the mini marshmallows. Set aside.

03 Put the white chocolate and speculoos spread (cookie butter) into a medium microwave-safe bowl and microwave on high in 30-second bursts, stirring at each interval, until melted. Alternatively, melt using a double boiler (see page 17).

04 Pour the melted chocolate mixture over the marshmallow mixture and stir with a wooden spoon or rubber spatula until everything is completely coated. Scoop into your prepared pan and press down evenly, then top with extra cookies, if using. Chill in the refrigerator for at least 1 hour until set.

05 To serve, remove from the refrigerator and let stand for about 10 minutes, then cut into 16 pieces.

06 Store in an airtight container in the refrigerator or at room temperature for up to 4 days.

119

Tray Bakes

COOKIES and CREAM MAGIC BARS

Makes 20

~~

These bars are just magical, hence the title. They're sweet, crunchy, gooey and chocolatey. There's no real mixing involved – you pretty much just chuck everything in the pan and bake!

45 minutes

10.5oz (300g) cream-
filled chocolate
sandwich cookies
(I use Oreos) +
20 broken cookies

7½ tbsp (110g) unsalted
butter, melted

1 x 14oz (397g) can
condensed milk

1⅓ cups (300g) white or
milk chocolate chips

01 Preheat the oven to 350°F/180°C (160°C fan)/Gas mark 4 and line a 8 x 10in (20 x 25cm) baking pan with parchment paper (see page 16).

02 Put the 10.5oz (300g) of cookies into a food processor and process until finely crushed. Alternatively, put them into a plastic bag and crush with a rolling pin. Tip into a medium bowl, then pour in the melted butter and mix together with a spoon until fully combined.

03 Scoop the mixture into your prepared pan and press down firmly with the back of a spoon. Pour over the condensed milk, then sprinkle over the chocolate chips and remaining broken cookies and press down with the back of a fork.

04 Bake for 30–35 minutes until the edges are crisp. Leave to cool completely in the pan, then cut into 20 bars.

05 Store in an airtight container in the refrigerator or at room temperature for up to 5 days.

SWAP:
~~

Swap the cookies
for speculoos cookies
and drizzle melted
speculoos spread
(cookie butter) on
top when cool.

GOOEY FLAPJACKS

Makes 16
~~

These chewy oat bars are always a winner for me, but they have to be soft and gooey, none of this crunchy, crumbly stuff that falls apart in your hands! These flapjacks are quick to make and taste absolutely delicious. You can easily add your favorite toppings or any extras, including spreads such as speculoos or chocolate.

30 minutes

5.25oz (150g) unsalted
  butter
⅔ cup (120g) light
  brown sugar
⅓ cup (80ml) honey
3½ cups (280g) rolled oats

01 Preheat the oven to 350°F/180°C (160°C fan)/Gas mark 4 and line an 8in (20cm) square baking pan with parchment paper (see page 16).

02 Put the butter, sugar and honey into a large saucepan and warm over a medium heat, stirring constantly with a wooden spoon, until the sugar dissolves and the mixture is fully combined. Turn off the heat, add the oats and stir until completely coated, then pour the mixture into your prepared pan and spread out evenly.

03 Bake for 20 minutes until the edges are crisp and golden brown but the middle is still wobbly (this is the secret to soft and gooey flapjacks). Leave to cool completely in the pan, then cut into 16 squares. Yum!

04 Store in an airtight container for up to 5 days.

TIP:
~~
Add a jam layer! Put half the oat mixture into the pan, spread over some jam and top with the rest of the mixture.

PEANUT BUTTER BLONDIES

Makes 16

~~

These are a must for peanut butter lovers! With only 5 ingredients, these blondies couldn't be easier. No eggs needed, just load it up with peanut butter cups or any extra add-ins for the ultimate peanut butter bake.

40 minutes

1 cup (200g) light
  brown sugar
4 tbsp (60ml) vegetable oil
¾ cup (185g) creamy
  peanut butter
1 cup (130g) all-purpose
  flour
¼ cup (60ml) milk, at room
  temperature

OPTIONAL EXTRAS
3oz (90g) mini peanut
  butter cups, chopped
3oz (90g) white chocolate,
  chopped into pieces

01 Preheat the oven to 350°F/180°C (160°C fan)/Gas mark 4 and line an 8in (20cm) square baking pan with parchment paper (see page 16).

02 Put the sugar, oil and peanut butter into a large mixing bowl and beat together with an electric hand mixer until smooth. Add the flour and fold in with a wooden spoon or rubber spatula until just combined, then pour in the milk and stir until smooth. If using, fold in the peanut butter cups and white chocolate now.

03 Pour the batter into your prepared pan and smooth it out to the edges. Bake for 25–30 minutes until the edges are golden and the middle still wobbles very slightly. Leave to cool completely in the pan (this will help the blondie to firm up), then cut into 16 squares. Enjoy!

04 Store in an airtight container at room temperature for up to 4 days.

SWAP:
~~
Swap the peanut butter cups for candy-coated chocolate buttons or chocolate chips, if you prefer.

NO-BAKE SPECULOOS SLICE

Makes 16

~~

You may have guessed that I'm totally speculoos obsessed, but this is one of my favorite tray bakes. It's so quick and so easy. The combination of speculoos and white chocolate is a dream. If you have a super sweet tooth like me, you will love this!

*20 minutes
+ 2 hours chilling*

3oz (90g) speculoos cookies (I use Biscoff)

2 generous cups (250g) powdered sugar

8½ tbsp (120g) unsalted butter, melted

Scant 1¼ cups (290g) speculoos spread/cookie butter (I use Biscoff)

7oz (200g) white chocolate, broken into pieces

01 Line an 8in (20cm) square baking pan with parchment paper (see page 16).

02 Put the cookies into a food processor and process until finely crushed. Alternatively, put into a plastic bag and crush with a rolling pin. Tip into a mixing bowl, then add the powdered sugar and melted butter and mix with a spoon until fully combined.

03 Add 1 cup (240g) of the speculoos spread (cookie butter) and mix together with a wooden spoon or rubber spatula until combined, then scoop into your prepared pan and press down firmly. Pop into the refrigerator while you prepare the topping.

04 Put the white chocolate into a microwave-safe bowl and microwave on high in 30-second bursts, stirring at each interval, until melted and smooth. Set aside.

05 Put the remaining speculoos spread into a separate microwave-safe bowl and microwave on high in 20-second bursts, stirring at each interval, until runny and smooth.

06 Remove the base from the refrigerator and pour over the melted white chocolate, spreading it out to the edges. Give the pan a shake for a smoother finish. Drizzle the melted speculoos spread over the top, then swirl a knife or skewer through the spread and chocolate to create a pretty pattern.

07 Chill in the refrigerator for at least 2 hours until set. To serve, remove the pan from the refrigerator and let it stand for about 10 minutes, then cut into 16 squares and enjoy!

08 Store in an airtight container in the refrigerator for up to 5 days.

SWAP:

~~

Instead of speculoos spread and cookies, use chocolate-hazelnut spread and graham crackers.

APPLE PIE BARS

Makes 16
~~

Who doesn't love apple pie? With only 5 ingredients, this bake is a total winner in my household. It's quick and easy to make and tastes amazing warmed up with ice cream or just as it is.

1 hour

2 cups (260g) self-raising flour

1 cup (200g) superfine sugar + 2 tbsp for sprinkling

3 large apples, peeled, cored and diced

4.5oz (130g) unsalted butter, melted and cooled

1 large egg

~~

Tray Bakes

01 Preheat the oven to 350°F/180°C (160°C fan)/Gas mark 4 and line an 8in (20cm) square baking pan with parchment paper (see page 16).

02 Put the flour and the 1 cup (200g) sugar into a large mixing bowl and mix together, then add the diced apples and toss until completely coated. Add the melted butter and egg and stir together with a wooden spoon until well combined.

03 Spoon the batter into your prepared pan and spread it out to the edges, then sprinkle over the 2 tablespoons of sugar for a sweet, crunchy top.

04 Bake for 40–45 minutes until golden brown and a toothpick inserted into the middle comes out clean. Leave to cool completely in the pan, then cut into 16 bars.

05 Store in an airtight container in the refrigerator or at room temperature for up to 4 days.

TIP:
~~
Add ground cinnamon to the apple mix for an extra burst of flavor!

TANGY LEMON BARS

Makes 16
~~

These bars are so fresh and tangy – perfect for a summer's day out in the garden. They're super easy to make and are sure to satisfy when you're in need of something sweet with a zing!

50 minutes

FOR THE SHORTBREAD
5.25oz (150g) unsalted
    butter, softened
6 tbsp (75g)
    granulated sugar
Generous 1½ cups (210g)
    all-purpose flour

FOR THE LEMON TOPPING
6½ tbsp (55g) all-purpose
    flour
1½ cups (300g)
    granulated sugar
4 large eggs
Scant ½ cup (100ml)
    lemon juice (the juice
    of about 2 lemons)

01 Preheat the oven to 350°F/180°C (160°C fan)/Gas mark 4 and line an 8 x 10in (20 x 25cm) baking pan with parchment paper (see page 16).

02 Put all the shortbread ingredients into a large mixing bowl and mix together with your hands until crumbly and completely combined. Tip into your prepared pan and press down firmly with your hands or the back of a spoon.

03 Bake for 15–20 minutes until light golden brown.

04 Meanwhile, put the flour and sugar for the topping in a separate bowl and stir together with a balloon whisk, then mix in the eggs and lemon juice until frothy and completely combined.

05 Remove the shortbread from the oven and carefully pour over the lemon topping, then return to the oven and bake for another 20 minutes until the topping no longer wobbles. Leave to cool completely in the pan, then cut into 16 bars, serve and enjoy! (I recommend chilling them in the refrigerator for 2 hours for a cleaner cut and firmer bars).

06 Store in an airtight container in the refrigerator for up to 5 days.

TIP:
~~

Once baked, dust the bars with powdered sugar.

NUTTY CARAMEL BARS

Makes 16 bars

~~

These bars are so satisfyingly crunchy! They're chocolatey, chewy and nutty, thanks to the caramel peanut chocolate candy bars. With just 5 simple ingredients, this dessert is quick and fun to make and it's absolutely delicious! Perfect for parties, picnics and afternoon snacks.

15 minutes + 3 hours chilling

9oz (250g) caramel peanut chocolate bars (I use Snickers), cut into small pieces

4.5oz (125g) unsalted butter

Scant 2 tbsp (30g) honey

4½ cups (120g) puffed rice cereal (I use Rice Krispies)

14oz (400g) milk chocolate, broken into pieces and melted (see page 17)

01 Line an 8in (20cm) square baking pan with parchment paper (see page 16).

02 Put 7oz (200g) of the caramel peanut chocolate bar pieces into a medium saucepan, along with the butter and honey. Warm over medium heat, stirring constantly with a wooden spoon, until melted (the mixture will still contain lumps from the chocolate bars).

03 Pour the puffed rice into a large heatproof mixing bowl, then pour over the melted chocolate bar mixture and mix together until completely combined. Spoon into your prepared pan and press down firmly with the back of the spoon.

04 Pour over the melted milk chocolate and spread it out to the edges, giving the pan a shake for a smooth finish. Top with the remaining chocolate bar pieces.

05 Chill in the refrigerator for at least 3 hours, or until set, then cut into 16 bars and serve.

06 Store in an airtight container at room temperature (not in the fridge) for up to 5 days.

SWAP:

~~

Swap the chocolate bars for caramel nougat chocolate bars, for an alternative gooey slice!

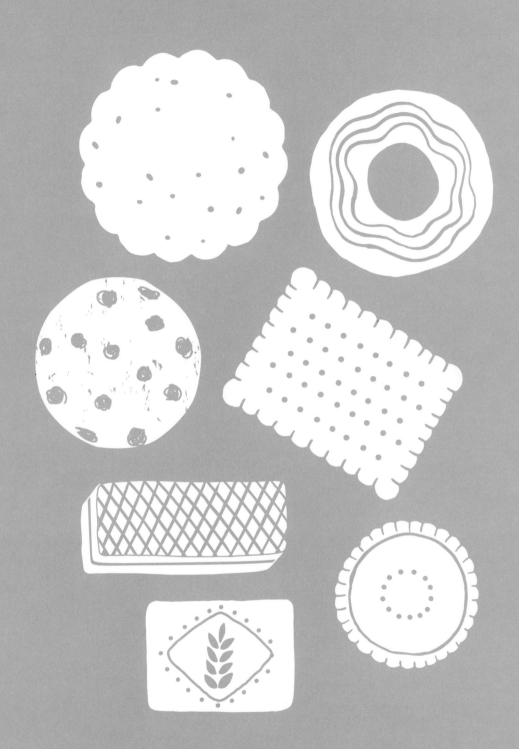

COOKIES
and
OTHER FLAT
BAKES

～

Chapter Five

I have a slight obsession with cookies

Anyone that knows me will tell you I have a slight obsession with cookies... they are so quick and easy to make, and I love that once you have a dough, you can pretty much add whatever you want to it. The options are endless.

In this chapter, you will find a mixture of speedy 3-ingredient cookies made with your favorite spreads, such as chocolate, peanut butter and speculoos (cookie butter), plus classics like chocolate chip shortbread. Yum!

Find my ultimate favorite **Chewy Chocolate Chip Cookies** and a **Stuffed Cookie Pie** in the All-Star Bakes chapter on pages 248 and 220.

So soft!

PEANUT BUTTER COOKIES

Makes 16

~

I couldn't write this book without including these super-easy cookies. They're soft, chewy and packed with peanut butter flavor – perfect for lunchboxes or with a cup of tea or coffee.

15 minutes

1 cup (250g) creamy
peanut butter
1 cup (200g) granulated
sugar + extra for sprinkling
1 large egg

01 Preheat the oven to 350°F/180°C (160°C fan)/Gas mark 4.

02 Put the peanut butter, sugar and egg into a large mixing bowl and mix together with a balloon whisk until smooth.

03 Scoop up 2 tablespoons of the mixture and roll into a ball, then place on a nonstick cookie sheet (see page 11) and flatten with the back of a fork to form a criss-cross pattern. Repeat with the remaining mixture to make about 16 cookies, spacing them at least 3in (7.5cm) apart on the sheet.

04 Bake for 8–9 minutes until the cookies look crisp and golden brown. Sprinkle with a little extra sugar and leave to cool on the sheet for at least 10 minutes, then transfer to a cooling rack to cool completely.

05 Store in an airtight container at room temperature for up to 4 days.

TIP:
~
Add chocolate chips or any other extras to the dough in Step 2 to make these cookies extra delicious!

CHOCOLATE HAZELNUT COOKIES

Makes 5

These may just be the quickest and easiest cookies you will ever make. They're soft, chewy and chocolatey and are great as a quick afternoon snack, or packed up in picnics and lunchboxes. Result!

15 minutes

5½ tbsp (100g) chocolate-hazelnut spread (I use Nutella)

7 tbsp (60g) all-purpose flour + extra if needed

2 tbsp milk + extra if needed

01 Preheat the oven to 350°F/180°C (160°C fan)/Gas mark 4.

02 Put all the ingredients into a small bowl and mix together with a spoon to form a dough. If it's still crumbly, add a tiny bit more milk; if it's sticky and wet, add a little extra flour.

03 Divide the dough into 5 equal pieces, then roll into balls and press them down slightly into a rough cookie shape on a nonstick cookie sheet (see page 11), spacing them about 3in (7.5cm) apart.

04 Bake for 8–9 minutes until the edges are lightly crisp. Leave to cool on the sheet for 10 minutes, then transfer to a cooling rack to cool completely. Enjoy!

05 Store in an airtight container at room temperature for up to 4 days.

Cookies & Other Flat Bakes

SWAP:

Replace the chocolate-hazelnut spread with speculoos spread (cookie butter) for a delicious alternative.

SOFT SPECULOOS COOKIES

Makes 6

~

If you love speculoos spread (cookie butter) and sweet, cinnamon flavors, these cookies are for you. Soft and chewy with crisp edges, they just melt in your mouth and you won't believe they're made with just 3 ingredients. White chocolate chips also taste amazing in them, if you have a bag to spare.

15 minutes

1¼ cups (300g) speculoos spread/ cookie butter (I use Biscoff)

⅔ cup (85g) all-purpose flour

1 large egg

01 Preheat the oven to 400°F/200°C (180°C fan)/Gas mark 6.

02 Put all the ingredients into a medium mixing bowl and mix together with a spoon to form a dough.

03 Divide into 6 equal pieces, then roll into balls and place on a nonstick cookie sheet (see page 11), spacing them at least 4in (10cm) apart.

04 Bake for 10 minutes until the edges are crisp and the cookies are lightly cracked on top. Leave to cool on the sheet for at least 10 minutes, then transfer to a cooling rack to cool completely.

05 Store in an airtight container at room temperature for up to 4 days.

SWAP:
~
Replace the speculoos spread with chocolate-hazelnut spread for the most amazing chocolate cookies!

TIP:
~
Fold in white choc chips or candy-coated chocolate buttons at Step 2 to make these cookies look and taste even better.

EASY JAM TARTS

Makes 12 tarts

~

There's nothing quite like a homemade jam tart, especially when it's fresh from the oven and still slightly warm. The best thing about these is you can use ready-rolled pastry dough and the tarts are ready to eat within about 30 minutes. You can use any jam you fancy or use a few different ones for variety. These are fab for tea parties and super easy to make with kids.

30 minutes

1 sheet (11oz/320g)
  ready-rolled shortcrust
  pastry dough (or two
  7oz/200g sheets of
  ready-rolled pie dough)
12 tsp jam of your choice
1 egg, beaten

01 Preheat the oven to 350°F/180°C (160°C fan)/Gas mark 4 and grease a 12-cup cupcake pan with butter or spray it with cooking oil.

02 Following the package directions, unroll the dough onto a clean, flat surface, then cut out 12 circles using a crinkle cookie cutter. The cookie cutter should be about 0.4in (1cm) bigger in diameter than your cupcake holes. Gently press each round into your prepared pan.

03 Add 1 teaspoon of your favorite jam to each tart. Be careful not to overfill them, as they may bubble over in the oven. Brush the edges of each tart with the beaten egg.

04 Bake for 10–12 minutes until the edges are light brown and the pastry is cooked through. Leave to cool in the pan for 10 minutes, then transfer to a cooling rack to cool completely. Have fun!

05 Store in an airtight container at room temperature for up to 4 days.

TIP:

~

Feel free to use any jam you like. Lemon curd or a similar spread will also taste delicious!

NO-BAKE CHOCOLATE TART

Serves 12

This tart is super rich and chocolatey. With a buttery graham cracker base and a dark chocolate ganache filling, no one will ever guess it's made with just 4 ingredients! It's perfect for dinner parties with friends and family.

20 minutes + 3 hours chilling

12.4oz (350g) graham crackers

6¼ ounces (180g) unsalted butter, melted

12oz (340g) dark chocolate chips or dark chocolate (at least 50% cocoa/cacao), broken into small pieces

1 cup (250ml) heavy cream

01 Grease a 9in (23cm) tart pan with removable bottom with butter.

02 Put the graham crackers into a food processor and process until finely crushed. Alternatively, put them into a plastic bag and crush with a rolling pin. Tip into a medium bowl, then pour in the melted butter and mix together until fully combined.

03 Press the mixture into your prepared pan using the base of a glass and your fingers to get it right to the edges, then pop it in the refrigerator while you make the filling.

04 Put the chocolate chips or chocolate pieces into a heatproof bowl. Put the cream into a microwave-safe jug and microwave on high for about 1 minute 20 seconds until hot, but not boiling. Pour the hot cream over the chocolate and leave to stand for about 2 minutes.

05 Gently stir the cream and chocolate until completely combined, thick and smooth. Remove the base from the refrigerator, then pour over the chocolate filling. Chill in the refrigerator for 3 hours, or until set (overnight is preferable).

06 To serve, pop the tart out of the pan and cut into 12 slices.

07 Store in the refrigerator for up to 4 days.

Serving suggestions

Serve with ice cream, berries, powdered sugar or caramel sauce and a sprinkle of salt for even more flavor.

SWAP:

Use cream-filled chocolate sandwich cookies for the base and reduce the butter to 5.25oz (150g) for double the chocolate!

4 INGREDIENTS · INGREDIENTS · INGREDIENTS · INGREDIENTS ·

CONDENSED MILK COOKIES

Makes 8

~

These cookies are sweet, buttery and melt in your mouth! They're perfect for picnics, afternoon teas and snacks in the garden. Change up the filling to make a different cookie each time – speculoos or chocolate-hazelnut spread, lemon curd, peanut butter or even melted chocolate are all great additions.

25 minutes + 30 minutes cooling

7½ tbsp (110g) cold unsalted butter, cubed

1⅓ cups (175g) all-purpose flour + extra if needed and for dusting

¼ cup (60ml) sweetened condensed milk

8 tsp jam of your choice

01   Preheat the oven to 350°F/180°C (160°C fan)/Gas mark 4.

02   Put the butter and flour into a large mixing bowl and rub together with your fingertips until the mixture is crumbly. Stir in the sweetened condensed milk, then mix together with your hands to form a soft dough, adding an 1 extra tablespoon of flour at a time if the dough is still sticky.

03   Tip the dough onto a floured surface, then roll out to about ¼in (5mm) thick. Using a small cookie cutter, cut out circles in the dough, then re-roll the trimmings and repeat to make 16. Using the base of a piping nozzle or small bottle cap, cut out a hole in the middle of half the circles. Place all the circles on a nonstick cookie sheet (see page 11), spacing them about 1in (2.5cm) apart.

04   Bake for 10 minutes until lightly golden, then leave to cool completely on the sheet.

05   Once cool, place a blob of your favorite jam in the center of the cookie bases (the ones without the holes), then place the cookie lids on the top. The jam will help secure the lids in place.

06   Store in an airtight container at room temperature for up to 4 days.

SWAP:

~

Swap the jam for lemon curd or your favorite spread such as speculoos, chocolate or peanut butter.

CHOCOLATE BRICKS

Makes 16
~~

If you had these at school, you won't need to read my description – you will already know. My school called them chocolate bricks and I used to eat one almost every break time, fresh out of the oven, soft and still slightly warm. They look like a chocolate brownie, but taste more like a soft chocolate shortbread. Absolutely delicious!

45 minutes

1½ cups (300g) granulated sugar + extra for sprinkling

½ cup + 2 tbsp (50g) cocoa powder

3 cups (400g) all-purpose flour

10.5oz (300g) margarine or butter, melted

01 Preheat the oven to 340°F/170°C (150°C fan)/Gas mark 3½ and line a 8 x 10in (20 x 25cm) baking pan with parchment paper (see page 16).

02 Put the sugar, cocoa powder and flour into a large mixing bowl and mix together with a balloon whisk until combined. Pour in the melted margarine or butter and stir together with a wooden spoon or rubber spatula to form a stiff dough.

03 Transfer the dough to your prepared pan and press down firmly with your hands or the back of a spoon. Brush the top with water, then sprinkle with a little extra sugar.

04 Bake for 30–35 minutes until the top is firm but still soft if pressed. Leave to cool completely in the pan, then cut into 16 bars. Enjoy!

05 Store in an airtight container at room temperature for up to 4 days.

TIP:
~~
Why not add chocolate chips or serve it with vanilla pudding.

AS SEEN ON GOOD MORNING AMERICA

CHOCOLATE CHIP SHORTBREAD BARS

Makes 16

This is a classic, soft and buttery shortbread—loaded with chocolate chips—with a sweet, crunchy crust. You barely even need instructions for this one, it's that easy. Best served with a cup of tea, coffee or a glass of cold milk. Perfection!

40 minutes

8oz (225g) unsalted butter, softened

9 tbsp (115g) granulated sugar + 2 tbsp for sprinkling

2½ cups (320g) all-purpose flour

9 tbsp (120g) dark or milk chocolate chips

01 Preheat the oven to 350°F/180°C (160°C fan)/Gas mark 4 and line an 8in (20cm) square baking pan with parchment paper (see page 16).

02 Put the butter, sugar and flour into a large mixing bowl and rub together with your fingertips until the mixture is completely combined and crumbly. Add 7 tbsp (90g) of the chocolate chips and fold in with a wooden spoon or rubber spatula until evenly distributed.

03 Transfer the dough to your prepared pan and press down firmly with your hands or the back of a spoon. Press the remaining chocolate chips into the top, then sprinkle over the 2 tablespoons of sugar for a crunchy topping.

04 Bake for 25–30 minutes until the edges are lightly golden and the top is firm but still soft if pressed. Leave to cool completely in the pan, then cut into 16 squares. Enjoy!

05 Store in an airtight container at room temperature for up to 4 days.

Cookies & Other Flat Bakes

TIP:

For a nice soft shortbread, don't overcook it. It should still be soft and light in color when it comes out of the oven.

CREAMY CHEESECAKE COOKIES

Makes 12

~~

All the flavors of a cookies and cream cheesecake, but in cookie form. It's like a dream come true – two of my favorite sweet things combined! They are soft, chewy and creamy, and you don't even need eggs.

20 minutes + 1 hour chilling

8 tbsp (115g) unsalted butter, softened

4oz (115g) full-fat cream cheese

1 cup (200g) granulated sugar

Scant 1 cup (120g) all-purpose flour

10 cream-filled chocolate sandwich cookies (I use Oreos), broken into small pieces

01 Preheat the oven to 350°F/180°C (160°C fan)/Gas mark 4.

02 Put the butter and cream cheese into a large mixing bowl and beat together with an electric hand mixer until creamy. Add the sugar and beat until combined, then fold in the flour with a wooden spoon or rubber spatula until just combined.

03 Add the broken cookies and fold in until evenly distributed, then cover the bowl with plastic wrap and chill in the refrigerator for 1 hour.

04 Scoop up about 2 tablespoons of the dough and place on a nonstick cookie sheet (see page 11). Repeat with the remaining dough to make 12, spacing them at least 4in (10cm) apart on the sheet.

05 Bake for 10 minutes until the edges are golden brown. Leave to cool on the sheet for 15 minutes, then transfer to a cooling rack to cool completely. Enjoy!

06 Store in an airtight container in the refrigerator for up to 3 days.

TIP:

~~

Be sure to use a good-quality cream cheese (I use Philadelphia) and pour off any excess liquid.

S'MORES TART

Makes 8 slices

~~

Marshmallows, melted chocolate, cinnamon and fresh, warm pastry.
This dessert is beyond easy to make, with no real mixing involved.
It's great to make with kids and perfect for any time of the year.

30 minutes

1 sheet (11oz/320g) of
  ready-rolled shortcrust
  pastry dough (or 2 x
  7oz/200g sheets of
  ready-rolled pie dough)
2 tbsp granulated sugar
1 tsp ground cinnamon
1lb (500g) milk chocolate
  bars (or enough to cover
  the tart)
40 marshmallows
  (or enough to cover
  the tart)

~~

Cookies & Other Flat Bakes

01 Preheat the oven to 400°F/200°C (180°C fan)/Gas mark 6
    and line a large sheet pan with parchment paper (or use a
    cookie sheet).

02 Following the package directions, unroll the pastry dough
    onto the prepared sheet pan. If your pastry comes in two
    smaller pieces, patch them together and trim as needed to
    get a rectangle measuring 14 x 9in (35 x 23cm). Fold in the
    edges of the dough to create a lip about scant ½in (1cm)
    wide, then bake for 10 minutes.

03 Meanwhile, mix together the sugar and cinnamon in a small
    bowl or mug.

04 Remove the pastry sheet from the oven, then evenly sprinkle
    over the cinnamon sugar. Arrange your chocolate bars to
    cover the pastry, then top with the marshmallows in rows,
    ensuring they stay within the pastry lip, or they may bubble
    over and create a mess in the oven.

05 Continue to bake for another 10–15 minutes until the
    marshmallows are crisp and golden brown on top and the
    pastry is cooked through. If you want to toast the top a little
    more, pop the tart under a preheated hot broiler for
    a couple of minutes or use a kitchen blowtorch.

06 Leave to cool for 5 minutes, then cut into 8 slices and serve.
    Enjoy!

TIP:
~~
You can also
make this in
a pizza oven!

ICE CREAMS, SHAKES and CHILLED DESSERTS

~~

Chapter Six

Silky, creamy and delicious

The recipes in this chapter were my favorite to test. Grab your heavy cream and sweetened condensed milk – if you fancy something silky, creamy and delicious, you are in the right place!

In this chapter, you'll find 3-ingredient ice creams, thick milkshakes, a 3-ingredient **Crème Brûlée**, 5-ingredient **Mini Cheesecakes** and a 4-ingredient **Speculoos Lasagne** (yes, you read that correctly). These recipes are perfect for summer or whenever you fancy something cool and refreshing. Here's a few tips when making them:

- **Use good-quality, full-fat cream cheese at room temperature** when making cheesecakes, and pour off any excess liquid. This ensures the cheesecake will set properly.

- **Make sure you use sweetened condensed milk**, not unsweetened or evaporated milk.

Dreamy

COOKIES and CREAM ICE CREAM

Serves 10

~~

Homemade ice cream couldn't be easier! You don't need any fancy equipment or ingredients. Just grab an electric hand mixer and a standard loaf pan or container and you're ready to go. This ice cream is really creamy and packed with flavor, which is great, because no one wants to be eating flavored ice!

15 minutes
+ 6 hours freezing

10.5oz (300g) cream-filled chocolate sandwich cookies (I use Oreos)

One 14oz (397g) can sweetened condensed milk

Scant 2 cups (475ml) cold heavy cream

01 Put the cookies into a bowl and roughly crush with your hands, or use a knife and chopping board. Set aside.

02 Pour the sweetened condensed milk and cream into a large mixing bowl and beat with an electric hand mixer until soft peaks form. Add 9oz (250g) of the crushed cookies and fold in with a rubber spatula or wooden spoon.

03 Scoop the mixture into a 9 x 5in (23 x 13cm) loaf pan or freezer-proof container, then smooth out evenly with the back of a spoon. Sprinkle over the remaining crushed cookies.

04 Double-wrap the entire loaf pan or container with plastic wrap, ensuring no moisture can get in, then freeze for at least 6 hours, or overnight if possible.

05 When ready to serve, remove the ice cream from the freezer and leave to stand for 5–10 minutes. Unwrap the pan or container, then dip an ice cream scoop into hot water (this makes serving the ice cream slightly easier) and scoop the ice cream into bowls.

06 Store in a sealed container in the freezer for up to 2 months.

SWAP:
~~

Try swapping the cream-filled chocolate sandwich cookies for a different type of cookie or a chocolate bar. Yum!

BLACKBERRIES *and* CREAM ICE CREAM

Serves 10

~~

Sweet, fruity and creamy, and with no ice-cream maker or fancy equipment needed, this ice cream is quick to prepare and makes enough to feed a hungry party of guests. It's best made the day before you want to serve it, so it can freeze overnight.

15 minutes
+ 6 hours freezing

14oz (400g) blackberries (fresh or frozen)
1 x 14oz (397g) can sweetened condensed milk
Scant 2 cups (475ml) cold heavy cream

01   Put the blackberries into a bowl and crush with the back of a fork. Set aside.

02   Put the sweetened condensed milk and cream into a large mixing bowl and beat with an electric hand mixer or stand mixer until soft peaks form and the mixture is super thick and creamy.

03   Add the crushed blackberries and fold in with a wooden spoon or rubber spatula. If you fold them through just a couple times, you will end up with a pretty marble effect. Keep folding to turn the ice cream completely purple.

04   Scoop the mixture into a 8 x 4in (20 x 10cm) loaf pan or freezer-proof container, then smooth out evenly with the back of a spoon. Double-wrap the entire pan or container in plastic wrap, ensuring no moisture can get in, then freeze for at least 6 hours, or overnight if possible.

05   When ready to serve, remove the ice cream from the freezer and leave to stand for 5–10 minutes. Unwrap the pan or container, then dip an ice cream scoop into hot water (this makes serving the ice cream slightly easier) and scoop the ice cream into bowls. Enjoy!

06   Store in a sealed container in the freezer for up to 2 months.

MANGO SORBET

Serves 6-8

~~~

This is the ultimate summer dessert. It's so fresh and fruity, and is beyond easy to make. If you love mango, you need to try this refreshing sorbet – it's bursting with mango flavors, with a tang of lime and extra sweetness from the maple syrup or honey.

15 minutes

1lb 5oz (600g) frozen mango chunks
4½ tbsp (70ml) maple syrup or honey
2 tbsp (30ml) fresh lime or lemon juice

01 Put the frozen mango into a blender or food processor and pulse until the chunks break up and form small shreds.

02 Scrape down the sides of the blender or food processor, then add the maple syrup or honey and lime or lemon juice and blend until smooth and creamy.

03 Serve immediately, or transfer to an airtight container and freeze for 2–3 hours for a firmer sorbet.

04 If serving from the freezer, leave to stand at room temperature for 10 minutes for easier scooping. So refreshing!

05 Store in a sealed container in the freezer for up to 3 weeks.

Ice Creams, Shakes & Chilled Desserts

Cookies and Cream
Milkshake

Salted Caramel
Milkshake

COOKIES and CREAM MILKSHAKE

Serves 2

This milkshake is thick, creamy and absolutely delicious – just like the kind you get at your favorite café or restaurant. It's perfect for a hot summer's day, or when you're curled up on the sofa in front of a movie. It's quick and easy to make, plus you can dress it up to look as fancy as you like.

5 minutes

6 cream-filled chocolate sandwich cookies (I use Oreos)
1 pint (450g) good-quality vanilla ice cream, softened
4 tbsp (60ml) milk (whole milk provides the creamiest flavor)

01 Put the cookies into a blender and pulse until roughly crushed.

02 Add the ice cream and milk and blend until smooth and creamy.

03 Pour into 2 glasses and serve with straws.

Serving suggestions

For a fancy version, top with whipped cream, add a cream-filled chocolate sandwich cookies and drizzle with chocolate sauce.

Ice Creams, Shakes & Chilled Desserts

SWAP:

You can try this with other cookies, such as cream-filled chocolate or vanilla sandwich cookies.

SEE THIS PICTURED ON THE PREVIOUS PAGE

SALTED CARAMEL MILKSHAKE

Serves 2

Salted caramel is one of my absolute favorite flavors, especially in a milkshake. This one is cool, creamy and refreshing, with a sweet and salty tang – yum! It's incredibly easy to make and feel free to add your favorite toppings.

5 minutes

1 pint (450g) good-quality vanilla or caramel ice cream, softened

4 tbsp (60ml) milk (whole milk provides the creamiest flavor)

6 tbsp salted caramel sauce (see page 52) + extra for drizzling

01 Put the ice cream, milk and salted caramel sauce into a blender and blend until smooth and creamy.

02 Drizzle extra salted caramel sauce around the inside of 2 tall glasses, if desired, then pour the milkshake into the glasses.

03 Add straws and serve drizzled with extra caramel sauce.

Serving suggestions

Try dressing up your milkshakes by topping them with whipped cream and sprinkling over butterscotch chips, chopped nuts or crushed cookies for extra flavor.

171

SWAP:

Instead of the salted caramel sauce, use chocolate sauce for a delicious chocolatey milkshake.

SEE THIS PICTURED ON THE PREVIOUS PAGE

CHOCOLATE MOUSSE

Serves 6

~

This is the perfect dessert for chocolate lovers. With just 3 basic ingredients, you can make a seriously indulgent, velvety and smooth chocolate mousse that is ideal for dinner parties and date nights. Why not make it for Valentine's Day and add a couple of strawberries? Delicious!

15 minutes
+ 15 minutes cooling and 2 hours chilling

¾ cup (170g) milk or dark chocolate chips
Scant 1 cup (225ml) cold heavy cream
4 tbsp (30g) powdered sugar

01 Put the chocolate chips and ½ cup (125ml) of the cream into a large microwave-safe bowl and microwave in 20-second bursts, stirring well at each interval. Leave to cool for about 15 minutes, stirring occasionally.

02 In another bowl, whip together the remaining cream and the powdered sugar with an electric hand mixer until stiff peaks form.

03 Fold the whipped cream into the cooled melted chocolate mixture with a rubber spatula until combined, keeping as much air in the mix as possible.

04 Scoop into 6 small ramekins or glasses, then chill in the refrigerator for at least 2 hours (the longer you chill them, the firmer they will be).

05 Store in an airtight container in the refrigerator for up to 3 days.

Serving suggestion ~~~~~~~~~~~~~~~~~~~~~~~~~~

Try these topped with chocolate shavings, strawberries and whipped cream.

TIP:
~
Dark chocolate chips make this mousse rich and firm; milk chocolate makes it more subtle and creamier.

SPECULOOS MOUSSE

Serves 4

~~

This mousse is silky, creamy and packed with sweet flavors. It's very easy to make, plus you can add any toppings you like to make it extra special.

10 minutes
+ 20 minutes chilling

1½ cups (375ml) cold heavy cream

Generous ¾ cup (200g) speculoos spread/cookie butter (I use Biscoff)

2 tbsp finely crushed speculoos cookies (I use Biscoff) + 2 cookies, halved (optional)

01 In a large mixing bowl, whip the cream using an electric hand mixer until stiff peaks form, then mix in ⅔ cup (150g) of the speculoos spread until combined. Spoon the chilled mousse into 4 small ramekins or glasses, then smooth out evenly with the back of the spoon. Chill in the refrigerator for 20 minutes.

02 Put the remaining speculoos spread into a microwave-safe bowl and microwave on high in 20-second bursts, stirring at each interval, then leave to cool slightly.

03 Drizzle one quarter of the melted spread over each mousse and gently smooth it across the top.

04 Sprinkle over the crushed cookies and decorate each mousse with a cookie half, if using. Enjoy!

05 These can be stored in an airtight container in the refrigerator for up to 3 days, but it's best to add the cookie half just before serving, or it will go soggy.

175
~~

Ice Creams, Shakes & Chilled Desserts

SWAP:
~~
Swap the speculoos spread for chocolate-hazelnut spread and top with marshmallows or hazelnuts.

NO-BAKE
VANILLA COOKIE CAKE

Serves 10
~~

This creamy cake is perfect for a hot day when you don't want to turn on the oven. It's packed with delicious cookies, which soften in the refrigerator to make an incredible no-bake cake. It's great to make a day ahead, then serve the next day at a BBQ or garden party. Your guests won't believe that it's made with just 3 ingredients! Once you've made this recipe, try it with different flavors of sandwich cookies.

20 minutes
+ 6 hours chilling

3 cups (750ml) cold
  heavy cream
6½ tbsp (50g) powdered
  sugar
57 cream-filled vanilla
  sandwich cookies
  (I use Golden Oreos)
  + 2 extra, crushed,
  for sprinkling

01 Line the bottom of a 9in (23cm) round springform cake pan with a circle of parchment paper (see page 16).

02 In a large mixing bowl, whip together the cream and powdered sugar with an electric hand mixer until stiff peaks form.

03 Spread a thin layer of the whipped cream over the bottom of your prepared pan (this helps to keep the cookies in place), then arrange one third of the cookies (you should use about 19) on top, making sure they sit tightly together. Gently spread one third of the cream over the cookies in a layer about scant ½in (1cm) thick. Repeat with the remaining ingredients to make 2 more layers, finishing with the cream.

04 Sprinkle the crushed cookies over the top, then chill in the refrigerator for at least 6 hours, or overnight if possible (chilling for this length of time ensures the cookies soften to a cake-like texture and the cake will be easier to cut into slices).

05 Carefully remove from the pan and transfer the cake to a serving plate, then cut into 10 slices using a sharp knife and serve. Enjoy!

06 Store in an airtight container in the refrigerator for up to 3 days.

CRÈME BRÛLÉE

Serves 2

~~

Crème brûlée at home has never been so easy – you'll feel like you're at a fancy restaurant! These are creamy, silky and smooth, with that crunchy, sugary crust that just makes a crème brûlée. They are perfect for dinner parties and special occasions, but try them midweek, too, just because you can!

1 hour
+ 10 minutes cooling,
3 hours chilling and
35 minutes standing

Scant ¾ cup (150g) good-quality vanilla ice cream
2 egg yolks
3 tbsp granulated sugar

01 Preheat the oven to 350°F/180°C (160°C fan)/Gas mark 4.

02 Put the ice cream into a microwave-safe bowl and microwave on high for about 40–50 seconds until melted, then leave to cool for about 10 minutes. Mix the egg yolks into the cooled melted ice cream with a balloon whisk until fully combined, then pour into 2 ramekins.

03 Place the ramekins in a baking pan, then pour hot water into the pan until it reaches about halfway up the sides of the ramekins. Carefully transfer to the oven and bake for about 45 minutes until set but still slightly wobbly in the middle.

04 Carefully remove the ramekins from the water bath and leave to cool, then chill in the refrigerator for at least 3 hours (they can be stored in the refrigerator at this point for up to 3 days).

05 When ready to serve, remove from the refrigerator and leave to stand for 30 minutes to let them reach room temperature.

06 Sprinkle half the sugar over each crème brûlée, then heat with a kitchen blowtorch until melted. If you don't have a torch, pop them under a preheated hot broiler until the sugar melts, keeping an eye on them so they don't burn. Leave to stand for 5 minutes until the sugar hardens. Enjoy!

~~

Ice Creams, Shakes & Chilled Desserts

SPECULOOS ICE CREAM

Serves 10

~~

This sweet and creamy homemade ice cream is a speculoos lover's dream. It's layered with thick swirls of speculoos spread and crunchy cookie pieces. Very simple to make, it's a winner in my household. Take the spoon away from me... In place of the speculoos spread and cookies, you could use peanut butter and mini peanut butter cups. Yum!

20 minutes
+ 6 hours freezing

1½ cups (350g) speculoos spread/cookie butter (I use Biscoff)

1 x 14oz (397g) can sweetened condensed milk

Scant 2 cups (475ml) cold heavy cream

3.5oz (100g) speculoos cookies (I use Biscoff), broken into small chunks

01 Put scant ½ cup (100g) of the speculoos spread into a microwave-safe bowl and microwave in 20-second bursts, stirring at each interval, until runny and smooth. Leave to cool.

02 Put the sweetened condensed milk, cream and the remaining speculoos spread into a large mixing bowl and beat with an electric hand mixer until soft peaks form. Add the broken cookies, reserving a handful to decorate, and fold in with a wooden spoon or rubber spatula.

03 Scoop one third of the cream mixture into a 9 x 5in (23 x 13cm) loaf pan or freezer-proof container, then smooth out evenly with the back of a spoon. Drizzle over one third of the melted spread, then swirl it through the ice cream with a knife or skewer. Repeat with the remaining ingredients to make 2 more layers, finishing with a swirl of melted spread.

04 Sprinkle over the reserved cookies, then double wrap the entire loaf pan or container with plastic wrap, ensuring no moisture can get in. Freeze for at least 6 hours, or overnight, if possible.

05 When ready to serve, remove the ice cream from the freezer and leave to stand for 5–10 minutes. Unwrap the pan or container, then dip an ice cream scoop into hot water (this makes serving the ice cream slightly easier) and scoop the ice cream into bowls.

06 Store in a sealed container in the freezer for up to 2 months.

STRAWBERRY ICEBOX CAKE

Serves 12

~

This is perfect for summer! Think warm BBQ out in the garden in the sunshine. You think you're too full for dessert, but this is brought to the table and suddenly your extra dessert stomach opens! It's creamy, yet light and fruity. Take 15 minutes to make it the day before, then pop it into the refrigerator until you're ready to serve.

15 minutes
+ 5 hours chilling

1⅔ cups (400ml) cold heavy cream

6½ tbsp (50g) powdered sugar

1lb (500g) strawberries, hulled and sliced ¼ inch (6mm) thick

6oz (170g) digestive biscuits or graham crackers

01 In a large mixing bowl, whip together the cream and powdered sugar with an electric hand mixer until soft peaks form.

02 Spread one third of the whipped cream over the bottom of an 11 x 7in (28 x 18cm) dish, smoothing it out evenly. Arrange one third of the biscuits over the cream, filling in any gaps with broken biscuits, then layer one third of the strawberry slices over the biscuits. Repeat with the remaining ingredients to make 2 more layers, finishing with strawberries.

03 Chill in the refrigerator for at least 5 hours, then serve and enjoy!

04 Store in the refrigerator for up to 3 days.

Ice Creams, Shakes & Chilled Desserts

SWAP:

~

Swap the strawberries for raspberries or blueberries for a different flavor.

SPECULOOS LASAGNE

Serves 8
~~

This dessert is so delicious! It's packed with speculoos-flavored cream, speculoos cookies and swirls of melted speculoos spread. It's perfect for serving to a crowd and there's no baking involved. The term 'lasagne' refers its layers, so don't worry, there's no pasta or meat involved! You might also liken it to a trifle.

20 minutes
+ 7 hours chilling

Generous ¾ cup (200g) speculoos spread/cookie butter (I use Biscoff)
1⅔ cups (400ml) cold heavy cream
6½ tbsp (50g) powdered sugar
25 speculoos cookies (I use Biscoff, and you may need more or less depending on your dish)

TO DECORATE
3½ tbsp (50g) speculoos spread/cookie butter
3 speculoos cookies,
  2 finely crushed
  + 1 left whole

SWAP:
~~
Try 30 cream-filled chocolate sandwich cookies and chocolate spread instead of speculoos cookies and spread.

01 To make the lasagne, put ⅔ cup (150g) of the speculoos spread (cookie butter) into a microwave-safe bowl and microwave in 20-second bursts, stirring at each interval, until runny and smooth. Leave to cool.

02 Put the cream, powdered sugar and the remaining 3½ tbsp (50g) of the speculoos spread into a large mixing bowl and beat with an electric hand mixer until stiff peaks form. Spread a thin layer of this whipped cream over the bottom of an 11 x 7in (28 x 18cm) dish (this helps to keep the cookies in place), then arrange a layer of cookies on top, making sure they sit tightly together. Drizzle half of the melted speculoos spread over the cookies. Gently spread half of the cream over the spread in a layer about scant ½in (1cm) thick, then repeat with the remaining cookies and melted spread. Finish with another layer of cream, smoothing it out evenly.

03 To decorate, melt and cool the speculoos spread as above, then pipe or drizzle over the lasagne, swirling it through the cream with a knife or skewer to make a pretty pattern. Sprinkle the cookie crumbs around the edge to form a border, then place a single cookie in the middle.

04 Chill in the refrigerator for at least 7 hours, or overnight (chilling for this length of time ensures the cookies soften and brings all the flavors together).

05 To serve, cut into 8 slices with a knife, then use a small metal spatula to get underneath all the layers and transfer onto plates or into bowls. Enjoy!

06 Store in the refrigerator, covered with plastic wrap or in a sealed container, for up to 3 days.

NO-BAKE COOKIES and CREAM CHEESECAKE

Serves 10

~

A show-stopping cheesecake with a buttery cookie base and a sweet, creamy filling loaded with cookie pieces. You could also swap the cream-filled chocolate sandwich cookies for a different flavor – why not try it with cream-filled vanilla sandwich cookies?

20 minutes
+ 6 hours chilling

FOR THE BASE
36 cream-filled chocolate
  sandwich cookies
  (I use Oreos)
6 tbsp (90g) unsalted
  butter, melted

FOR THE FILLING
Scant 2 cups (450ml) cold
  heavy cream
1lb (500g) full-fat
  cream cheese
1 cup (120g) powdered
  sugar
14 cream-filled chocolate
  sandwich cookies, broken
  into pieces + 5 extra,
  halved, to decorate

01 Line the bottom of an 8in (20cm) round springform cake pan with a circle of parchment paper (see page 16).

02 To make the base, put the cookies into a food processor and process until finely crushed. Alternatively, put into a plastic bag and crush with a rolling pin. Tip them into a medium bowl, then pour in the melted butter and mix together with a spoon until fully combined.

03 Transfer one third of the mixture to a separate bowl and set aside for the topping. Press the remaining mixture firmly into the bottom of your prepared pan, then pop into the refrigerator while you make the filling.

04 In a large mixing bowl, whip the cream with an electric hand mixer until stiff peaks form. In a separate bowl, beat together the cream cheese and powdered sugar with the electric mixer until creamy and smooth, then fold in the whipped cream with a rubber spatula until fully combined. Add the broken cookies and fold in.

05 Remove the chilled base from the refrigerator, then spoon in the filling, smoothing it out to the edges. Top with the reserved cookie crumb mixture, spreading it evenly over the top and pressing it down gently so it sticks. Decorate around the edge with the halved cookies. Chill in the refrigerator for at least 6 hours, or overnight, if possible, until set.

06 To serve, remove the cheesecake from the pan and transfer to a serving plate or board. Cut into 10 slices. Enjoy!

07 Store in the refrigerator for up to 4 days.

EASY MINI CHEESECAKES

Makes 12

~~

These gorgeous little cheesecakes are really easy to make and so versatile – you can dress them up or keep them nice and simple. Smooth, creamy and with a buttery graham cracker base, they are perfect for days in the sunshine and quick evening desserts.

15 minutes
+ 3 hours chilling
(or 20 minutes freezing)

FOR THE BASE
7oz (200g) graham crackers
4 tbsp (60g) unsalted butter, melted

FOR THE FILLING
11oz (320g) full-fat cream cheese, at room temperature
⅔ cup (160ml) cold heavy cream
Generous ¾ cup (100g) powdered sugar

01 Line a 12-cup muffin pan with cupcake liners.

02 To make the base, put the graham crackers into a food processor and process until finely crushed. Alternatively, put them into a plastic bag and crush with a rolling pin. Tip into a medium bowl, then pour in the melted butter and mix together with a spoon until fully combined. Spoon evenly into your cupcake liners, then press down firmly. Pop into the refrigerator while you make the filling.

03 Put the cream cheese, cream and powdered sugar into a large mixing bowl and beat with an electric hand mixer until stiff peaks form.

04 Remove the pan from the refrigerator and divide the filling between the liners, then smooth out evenly with the back of a spoon. Chill in the refrigerator for at least 3 hours, or until set. In a rush? You can freeze them for 20 minutes instead.

05 Store in an airtight container in the refrigerator for up to 3 days.

Serving suggestions ～～～～～～～～～～～～

Why not decorate your cheesecakes with a fresh strawberry or fresh berries, or go chocolatey and top with a square of chocolate, or even melted chocolate spread?

NO-BAKE
CHOCOLATE HAZELNUT
CHEESECAKE BARS

Makes 16
~

These cheesecake bars are thick, chocolatey and ultra-indulgent. They have a sweet, buttery cookie base and a smooth chocolate-hazelnut filling. They only take 15 minutes to make, then just pop them into the refrigerator to set before serving.

Ice Creams, Shakes & Chilled Desserts

15 minutes
+ 6 hours chilling

FOR THE BASE
10oz (280g) cream-filled chocolate sandwich cookies (I use Oreos) + 8 extra, halved, to decorate
7 tbsp (100g) unsalted butter, melted

FOR THE FILLING
1lb (500g) cream cheese
1⅓ cups (400g) chocolate-hazelnut spread (I use Nutella)
Generous ½ cup (70g) powdered sugar

01 Line an 8in (20cm) square baking pan with parchment paper (see page 16).

02 To make the base, put the cookies into a food processor and process until finely crushed. Alternatively, put them into a plastic bag and crush with a rolling pin. Tip into a medium bowl, then pour in the melted butter and mix together with a spoon until fully combined.

03 Press the mixture firmly into the bottom of your prepared pan, then pop into the refrigerator while you make the filling.

04 Put the cream cheese, chocolate-hazelnut spread and powdered sugar into a large mixing bowl and beat with an electric hand mixer until smooth and creamy.

05 Remove the chilled base from the refrigerator, then spoon in the filling, smoothing it out to the edges. Decorate with the halved cookies, then chill in the refrigerator for at least 6 hours, or overnight, if possible, until set. Cut into 16 squares to serve.

06 Store in the refrigerator for up to 3 days.

SWAP:
~

Instead of cream-filled chocolate sandwich cookies, you could use graham crackers.

SWEET
BREAKFASTS

~

Chapter Seven

The best meal of the day, if you ask me...

Ah, breakfast: the best meal of the day, if you ask me, and I like my breakfast sweet. You would have never guessed, would you?

This chapter is packed with breakfast basics, including 3-ingredient pancakes and crêpes and 4-ingredient **French Toast**, plus easy fruity bakes, such as **Apple Pie Parcels** and **Banana Oat Breakfast Cookies**.

Whether you're looking for something to make ahead and take on the go, or you want to whip up a quick weekend brunch for the family with a selection of toppings, there's something in this chapter for you.

Add your favorite fruits and syrups, go chocolatey and indulgent, or keep it sweet and simple. These recipes are so versatile, you can have a different variation every day.

Breakfast of dreams

BANANA PANCAKES

Serves 1

~~

These pancakes are perfect if you're looking for something quick, easy and delicious to set you up for the day. They're super versatile and will taste good with pretty much any toppings you wish, from peanut butter and sliced banana to mixed berries and maple syrup. Perfect for hungry kids and adults!

20 minutes

1 very ripe large banana
1 large egg
2½ tbsp (20g)
   self-raising flour

01   Put the banana into a medium bowl and mash with the back of a fork until smooth. Add the egg and mix in with a balloon whisk until fully combined, then fold in the flour with a wooden spoon or rubber spatula until just combined. Do not overmix, or you will end up with tough, rubbery pancakes.

02   Heat a nonstick frying pan over a medium heat and spray with cooking oil (you could use coconut oil, if you have it) or add a blob of butter, if you prefer.

03   Spoon one quarter of the batter into the middle of the pan and cook for about 2 minutes, or until bubbles appear on the top. Using a large spatula, flip it over and cook on the other side for 2 minutes until both sides are golden brown, then remove to a plate and keep warm. Repeat with the remaining batter to make 4 pancakes.

04   Serve with whatever you wish. Enjoy!

196

Sweet Breakfasts

TIP:
~~

Add a pinch of ground cinnamon or vanilla extract to the pancake batter for extra flavor.

EASY 3-INGREDIENT PANCAKES

Makes 10

These 3-ingredient pancakes are a staple in my household. They're cheap and easy to make, plus you can dress them up and flavor them however you wish. Perfect for lazy weekend breakfasts, the whole family will love them.

10–40 minutes (depending on how many batches)

2 large eggs
1 cup (250ml) milk
2⅓ cups (300g) self-raising flour

01 Put the eggs and milk into a medium bowl and mix together with a balloon whisk until fully combined. Add the flour and mix in until the batter is smooth.

02 Heat a large nonstick frying pan over a medium heat and spray with cooking oil or add a blob of butter.

03 Pour about ¼ cup (60ml) of the batter into the pan and cook for 1–2 minutes until bubbles appear on the top. You can cook them one at a time, or in batches if you have a griddle pan or a larger frying pan. Using a large spatula, flip over and cook on the other side for 1–2 minutes until golden brown. Repeat with the remaining batter to make 10 pancakes.

04 Serve each pancake immediately, with your favorite toppings (see below for suggestions).

Topping suggestions ～～～～～～～～～～

Try these delicious topping combinations: butter and maple syrup, lemon and sugar, berries and yogurt, fresh fruit and whipped cream, or even chocolate-hazelnut spread or speculoos spread (cookie butter).

TIP:

Fold any extras, such as chocolate chips or blueberries, into the batter at the end of Step 1 for extra flavor.

PEANUT BUTTER BREAKFAST BARS

Makes: 16

~

These bars are perfect for breakfast or when you are on the go – take them to work, pop them in lunchboxes or enjoy them before or after a workout. They are sweet, nutty and so tasty. The best part is, you don't even need to bake them – just store in the refrigerator and they're ready for when you need a burst of energy or are super hungry!

10 minutes + 30 minutes chilling

3 cups (240g) rolled oats
Scant 1 cup (240g)
  creamy peanut butter
Scant ½ cup (120ml) honey
  or maple syrup

01 Line an 8in (20cm) square baking pan with parchment paper (see page 16).

02 Put the oats into a large mixing bowl.

03 Put the peanut butter and honey or maple syrup into a medium saucepan and warm over a low–medium heat, stirring constantly with a wooden spoon, until smooth and combined. Pour over the oats and stir together until completely combined.

04 Press the mixture firmly into your prepared pan with your hands or the back of a spoon (press down as hard as possible so the bars are nice and compact).

05 Pop the pan into the freezer for 30 minutes or the refrigerator for 2–3 hours until set, then cut into 16 bars.

06 Store in an airtight container in the refrigerator for up to 1 week.

201

~

Sweet Breakfasts

SWAP:
~

Replace the peanut butter with another nut butter or a nut-free butter, such as sunflower seed.

PEANUT BUTTER BANANA SMOOTHIE

Serves 4

〜

Smoothies are great if you are in a rush or in need of a refreshing pick-me-up. Banana and peanut butter is always a winning combo for me – filling and super delicious. All you need is a blender and pre-frozen banana pieces, and in less than 5 minutes you have the perfect smoothie!

4 minutes
+ 2 hours freezing

2 bananas, cut into pieces and frozen
Scant 2 tbsp (30g) peanut butter (crunchy or smooth)
Generous 2 cups (500ml) milk

01   You can buy frozen bananas in a bag or freeze your own. If freezing your own, cut the bananas into scant ½in (1cm) pieces, separate into the portion sizes you require and freeze for about two hours.

02   Put all the ingredients into a blender and blend until smooth and creamy. You can also add a handful of frozen berries for extra flavor and fruitiness.

03   Divide between 4 glasses and serve – easy as that!

TIP:
〜
For a chocolatey version, add 1 tablespoon cocoa powder or hot chocolate powder.

APPLE PIE PARCELS

Makes 3

~

A fresh, warm pastry in the morning is always a good way to start the day. These little parcels are packed with a sweet, soft apple filling and topped with a sugary crust. Use any apple you wish: Granny Smith apples have a tarter taste while Pink Lady apples are sweeter. Serve these for breakfast at home or on the go, or try them warm with whipped cream for dessert.

30 minutes + 5 minutes cooling

1 large apple (about 11oz/320g), peeled, cored and cut into 16 slices

2½ tbsp superfine sugar + extra for sprinkling

1 sheet frozen puff pastry, thawed

01 Preheat the oven to 400°F/200°C (180°C fan)/Gas mark 6.

02 Put the apple slices and 1 teaspoon water into a saucepan, then cover with the lid and cook over a medium heat for 5 minutes until softened. Remove from the heat, then stir in the sugar and leave to cool.

03 Unroll the puff pastry sheet onto a clean, flat surface. Gently roll the dough into a rectangular shape. With a long edge facing you, cut the dough in half horizontally, then cut vertically to create 6 equal squares.

04 Brush the borders of 3 of the rectangles with water, then spoon one third of the cooled apple into the center of each. Place the remaining rectangles on top of each one, then seal the edges with the back of a fork. Make 3 small slits across the top of each, then sprinkle with sugar. For a golden glaze on the pastry, brush the tops with beaten egg before sprinkling over the sugar.

05 Transfer to a nonstick cookie sheet or a sheet pan lined with parchment paper, then bake for 15–20 minutes until the tops are golden brown and the pastry is cooked through. Leave to cool for 5 minutes before eating, as the apple filling will be very hot.

06 Store in an airtight container for up to 3 days.

TIP:
~
Add ½ teaspoon ground cinnamon to the apples for extra flavor and deliciousness.

BANANA OAT BREAKFAST COOKIES

Makes 12

These cookies are beyond easy to make and perfect for a quick breakfast or snack on the go. Packed with bananas, oats and chocolate chips, it's like eating a bowl of banana oatmeal, but in cookie form! They are soft, satisfying and oh so chocolatey.

10 minutes
+ 20 minutes chilling

1¼ cups (100g) old-fashioned rolled oats

5.25oz (150g) medium overripe bananas (weight without skin), mashed with the back of a fork until puréed

6 tbsp (80g) milk or dark chocolate chips

01   Preheat the oven to 350°F/180°C (160°C fan)/Gas mark 4.

02   Put a scant ⅔ cup (50g) of the oats into a food processor and pulse about 5 times until slightly powdery. Alternatively, you can crumble them between your fingertips int a bowl.

03   Put the bananas into a medium bowl with the broken-down oats and the remaining whole oats. Mix with a spoon until the mixture resembles a thick cookie batter. Fold in the chocolate chips.

04   Scoop up about 2 tablespoons of the mixture and press into an approximate cookie shape. Transfer to a cookie sheet or a sheet pan lined with parchment paper, then repeat with the remaining mixture to make 12 cookies.

05   Bake for 12–14 minutes until lightly golden and no longer looking wet. Leave to cool on the sheet for 15 minutes, then transfer to a cooling rack. Leave to cool completely. Enjoy!

06   Store in an airtight container for up to 3 days or freeze for up to 3 months.

Sweet Breakfasts

TIP:

Why not add 1 tsp ground cinnamon to the mixture for extra flavor?

SWAP:

Replace the milk or dark chocolate chips with dried fruit, chopped nuts or white chocolate chips.

EASY CRÊPES

Makes 10

~~

Crêpes make a delicious breakfast or dessert. They can be folded or rolled, and even stuffed with chocolate spread and strawberries. Yum! This recipe doesn't include sugar, so they can be served sweet or savory. Whip up a batch and serve immediately, or save them for later. With just 3 ingredients, these crêpes are perfect to feed a crowd and to eat at any time of the day.

30-40 minutes

2 cups (500ml) milk
2 large eggs
Scant 2 cups (250g) all-
    purpose flour

01   Put the milk and eggs into a large mixing bowl and mix together with a balloon whisk until fully combined, then mix in the flour until smooth.

02   Heat a nonstick frying pan over a medium heat and spray with cooking oil or add a small blob of butter.

03   Pour ⅓ cup (80ml) of batter into the pan, swirling it round to thinly and evenly coat the bottom of the pan. Cook for 1–2 minutes until the edges are crisp and start to lift, and the batter no longer looks wet on top, then slide a rubber spatula underneath the middle of the crêpe, lift it up and quickly flip it over. Cook on the other side for 1–2 minutes until light brown. Repeat with the remaining batter to make 10 crêpes.

04   Serve each crêpe immediately, with your favorite toppings (see below for suggestions).

05   These are best served fresh, but any leftovers can be stored in the refrigerator for up to 5 days. Reheat in a nonstick frying pan or in the microwave.

Topping suggestions ~~~~~~~~~~~~~~~~~~~~~

Some of my favorites are: lemon and sugar, chocolate-hazelnut spread, cinnamon sugar, maple syrup, honey, bananas or strawberries.

EASY FRENCH TOAST

Serves 4

~

French toast is one of my favorite breakfasts ever, and this recipe is sure to be a massive hit. I love how quick and easy it is to make and the toppings you can have with it are almost endless. A personal favorite of mine is peanut butter and warm mixed berries, with lots of honey. You can use any bread you want – I love challah bread, but brioche or just standard thick sliced bread also work perfectly. It helps if the bread is a couple of days old, so don't feel you need to go out and get a new loaf. Make this for the whole family or for yourself (just reduce the quantities).

30 minutes

3 large eggs
Scant 1 cup (230ml) milk
8 thick slices of bread
1 tbsp butter + more as needed

01 Put the eggs and milk into a large, shallow dish and mix together with a balloon whisk or fork until fully combined.

02 Working in batches, arrange some of the bread slices in a layer in the egg mixture and leave to soak for 2 minutes, then flip over and soak for 2 minutes on the other side.

03 Heat the butter in a large frying pan over a medium heat. Remove the bread slices from the egg mixture with a large spatula, letting any excess mixture drip off, then add to the pan and fry for 2 minutes until crisp and golden. Flip the slices over and cook on the other side for 2 minutes. Repeat with the remaining bread slices, adding a little more butter to the pan if needed.

04 Serve the French toast immediately with the toppings of your choice (see below for suggestions).

Topping suggestions ~~~~~~~~~~~~

Try serving these with your French toast: butter and maple syrup, powdered sugar, banana and honey, peanut butter and jam or fresh berries, chocolate-hazelnut spread or speculoos spread, cinnamon sugar, or whipped cream and fresh fruit.

TIP:
~
Add 1 tsp vanilla extract and 1 tsp ground cinnamon to the egg mixture. For sweetness, add 1 tbsp sugar.

ALL-STAR BAKES

~~

Chapter Eight

All my faves

Welcome to the chapter of the book that I just couldn't leave out. These bakes all have more than 5 ingredients, but they are **SO** worth it.

Here you will find a selection of my most popular recipes, including **Red Velvet Brownies** with cream cheese frosting, **No-bake White Chocolate Cheesecake, Chocolate Chip Cookie Dough Bars, Hot Chocolate Pudding, Cinnamon Swirl Banana Bread** and **Fudgy Triple Chocolate Brownies**.

Don't worry, they are all still really easy to make – they just take slightly more time and a little extra effort, but we've got this! Whether you love chocolate, lemon or cinnamon, there's something extra special in this chapter that you will love.

Not one to miss!

RAINBOW CUPCAKES

Makes 12

~~

These are the ultimate party cakes – bright and colorful, always the star of the show. I first made them to celebrate Pride month, and I was so pleased with how pretty they were and how surprisingly easy they were to make! The cake is a moist vanilla sponge, topped with a luscious, creamy vanilla buttercream – a classic and delicious combination, perfect for any occasion.

**50 minutes
+ 30 minutes cooling**

FOR THE CAKE BATTER
8oz (225g) margarine or
   unsalted butter, softened
Generous 1 cup (225g)
   superfine sugar
4 large eggs, lightly beaten
1¾ cups (225g) self-raising
   flour
1 tsp baking powder
1 tsp vanilla extract
2 tbsp whole milk
Purple, blue, green, yellow,
   orange and red strong
   food colorings (use
   high-quality brands
   like Sugarflair or Wilton;
   supermarket food
   colorings will not work)

FOR THE BUTTERCREAM
8½ tbsp (120g) unsalted
   butter, softened
1 tsp vanilla extract
2 cups (240g) powdered
   sugar
1 tbsp milk

4 tbsp rainbow cake
   sprinkles, to decorate

01   Preheat the oven to 350°F/180°C (160°C fan)/Gas mark 4 and line a 12-cup muffin pan with cupcake liners.

02   Put all the cake batter ingredients except the food colorings into a large mixing bowl and beat with an electric hand mixer for about 2–3 minutes until smooth. Divide the batter evenly between 6 small bowls, then add the purple food coloring to 1 batch of the batter and stir until you reach your desired color. Repeat with the remaining food colorings and batches of cake batter.

03   Transfer each colored cake batter into a separate disposable piping bag and cut off the tip. Pipe a layer of purple batter into each cupcake liner, then repeat with the others, 1 layer at a time, in the order they are listed in the ingredients (I found piping the batter the easiest way method, but if you prefer, you can spoon each color into the liners, smoothing out each layer with the back of a spoon before adding the next.)

04   Bake for 20–23 minutes until a toothpick inserted into the middle comes out clean. Leave to cool completely.

05   When the cakes are cool, make the buttercream. Put the butter into a large mixing bowl and beat with an electric hand mixer until light in color, then beat in the vanilla extract. Sift in half of the powdered sugar and beat until combined, then add the remaining powdered sugar and milk and beat until smooth and creamy.

06   Transfer the buttercream to a clean piping bag fitted with a star nozzle, then pipe onto the cooled cupcakes. Decorate each one with rainbow sprinkles.

07   Serve immediately or store in an airtight container for up to 3 days.

S'MORES COOKIE DOUGH BARS

Makes 16

~~

Soft cookie dough, loaded with graham cracker pieces, stuffed with chocolate bars and gooey marshmallow – these bars are a dream come true! Just try not to eat all the marshmallow spread before you need it...

1 hour
+ 3 hours chilling

FOR THE COOKIE DOUGH

8oz (225g) unsalted butter, softened

¾ cup (150g) light brown sugar

6 tbsp (75g) granulated sugar

2 large eggs

1 tsp vanilla extract

2 cups (270g) all-purpose flour

1 tsp baking soda

1 tsp salt

Scant 1 cup (200g) chocolate chips + 1½ tbsp (20g) for sprinkling

3.5oz (100g) graham crackers, broken into pieces

2 x 7oz (200g) milk chocolate bars

2 cups (200g) marshmallow spread (I use Marshmallow Fluff)

01 Preheat the oven to 340°F/170°C (150°C fan)/Gas mark 3½ and line a 9in (23cm) square baking pan with parchment paper (see page 16).

02 To make the cookie dough, put the butter and both sugars into a large mixing bowl and beat together with an electric hand mixer until light and fluffy. Add the eggs and vanilla extract and beat in with a wooden spoon until just combined (the mixture will look lumpy). Add the flour, baking soda and salt and fold in until only a few streaks of flour remain, then fold in the chocolate chips and graham cracker pieces until evenly distributed.

03 Scoop half the cookie dough into your prepared pan and smooth it out to the edges. Place the chocolate bars on top, then spoon over the marshmallow spread and gently smooth out evenly, leaving a ¾in (2cm) gap around the edges. Top with the remaining cookie dough and gently smooth out evenly, making sure there's no marshmallow spread peeking through. Sprinkle with the extra chocolate chips, if using.

04 Bake for 35–45 minutes until the top is golden brown and the middle no longer wobbles. Leave to cool completely in the pan, then chill in the refrigerator for at least 3 hours.

05 When ready to serve, remove from the refrigerator and leave to stand for about 10 minutes (this makes the chocolate easier to cut through; using a hot, sharp knife (see page 11) will also give you a cleaner cut). Cut into 16 bars and enjoy!

06 Store in an airtight container in the refrigerator for up to 4 days.

STUFFED COOKIE PIE

Serves 12
~~

Soft, caramel-y, loaded with chocolate chips and stuffed with chocolate spread. It doesn't get more indulgent! There's something about eating a warm slice of cookie with a spoon... yum! You could also add white chocolate chips and stuff it with speculoos spread, peanut butter, cream-filled chocolate sandwich cookies – let your imagination run wild.

45 minutes

7oz (200g) unsalted butter, softened

1¼ cups (250g) light brown sugar

1 large egg

1 tsp vanilla extract

2½ cups (320g) all-purpose flour

½ tsp baking soda

9 tbsp (120g) milk or dark chocolate chips

1 cup (300g) chocolate spread

Ice cream, to serve (optional)

01   Preheat the oven to 350°F/180°C (160°C fan)/Gas mark 4. Grease an 8in (20cm) round springform cake pan and line the bottom with a circle of parchment paper (see page 16).

02   Put the butter and sugar into a large mixing bowl and beat together with an electric hand mixer until light and fluffy. Add the egg and vanilla extract and mix in until just combined. Fold in the flour and baking soda with a wooden spoon or rubber spatula until only a few streaks of flour remain, then fold in 7 tbsp (100g) of the chocolate chips until evenly distributed.

03   Place one third of the dough on a piece of plastic wrap and press into an 8in (20cm) disc to form a lid. Set aside.

04   Press the remaining cookie dough into your prepared pan, creating a lip around the edge about 2in (5cm) high (I find this easiest to do with my fingertips). Spoon the chocolate spread into the middle and smooth it out to the edges using the back of the spoon, leaving about a scant ½in (1cm) gap around the top. Carefully place your cookie lid on the top and seal the edges with your fingers. Press the remaining chocolate chips into the lid.

05   Bake for 20–30 minutes until the top and edges are crisp and lightly golden. Leave to cool fully in the pan.

06   Once cool, transfer to a serving plate. To serve warm, reheat the whole pie in the oven at 340°F/170°C (150°C fan)/ Gas mark 3½ for 5 minutes. Alternatively, heat each slice individually in the microwave on medium for 20-30 seconds. Serve with a scoop of ice cream and dig in with a spoon!

07   Store in an airtight container for up to 4 days.

SWAP:
~~
Swap 2½ tbsp (20g) of the flour with ¼ cup (20g) cocoa powder to make a chocolatey cookie pie.

RED VELVET CAKE BALLS

Makes about 30

~~

If you have tried cake pops before, you'll know how amazing they taste. These balls are basically cake pops without the stick, although you could easily add a stick if you want. Mixed with cream cheese frosting (one of the best combinations with red velvet cake ever) and wrapped in creamy white chocolate – it doesn't get much better than this. They're great to store in the refrigerator for little bites of pure heaven, or take them to a party and watch them get demolished instantly! They're very easy to make and this method works with any cake and frosting combo. I've used a packaged cake mix, but feel free to make your own red velvet cake if you prefer.

1 hour
+ 1 hour cooling and
2 hours 20 minutes
chilling

1 x 15oz (425g) box red velvet cake mix + the ingredients on the box
Strong red food coloring (optional)
½ cup (150g) Cream Cheese Frosting (see page 225)
9oz (250g) white chocolate, broken into pieces

SWAP:

~~

Use chocolate cake and buttercream and swap the white chocolate for milk chocolate – delicious!

01 Preheat the oven to 350°F/180°C (160°C fan)/Gas mark 4 and line a 8 x 10in (20 x 25cm) baking pan with parchment paper (see page 16).

02 Make your red velvet cake batter following the package directions. I like to add a little extra red food coloring, but this is optional. Pour the batter into your prepared pan and smooth out evenly with the back of a spoon. Bake for 25–30 minutes until a toothpick inserted into the middle comes out clean. Leave to cool completely in the pan.

03 When cool, crumble the cake into fine crumbs in the pan with a fork or your hands. Set aside 2 tablespoons of the crumbs in a small bowl for decoration, then transfer the remaining crumbs to a large mixing bowl. Add the cream cheese frosting to the large bowl and fold in until a thick dough forms.

04 Line a sheet pan with parchment paper. Scoop up 1 tablespoon of the crumb dough, then roll into a ball with your hands and place on the prepared sheet pan. Repeat with the remaining mixture to make about 30 balls, then transfer to the freezer and chill for 20 minutes.

05 When ready to coat, set a cooling rack over a sheet of parchment paper and melt the chocolate (see page 17). Using 2 forks, coat each ball in the melted chocolate, letting any excess drip off, then transfer to the prepared cooling rack and sprinkle over the reserved cake crumbs.

06 Leave to set at room temperature or chill in the refrigerator for 1–2 hours until set. Carefully pop them off the cooling rack (you don't want to crack the chocolate) and serve. Enjoy!

07 Store in an airtight container in the refrigerator for up to 3 days.

RED VELVET BROWNIES

Makes 16
~~

These brownies are sure to please a crowd, especially if that crowd has a sweet tooth! They're bright red in color and topped with a sweet cream cheese frosting, perfect for Christmas or Valentine's Day, or any day of the year for that matter. You won't need any excuse to make these brownies over and over again. Feel free to halve the quantities for the frosting if you prefer a thinner layer. They also taste great without any frosting.

50 minutes
+ 2 hours cooling

FOR THE BROWNIES
6oz (170g) unsalted butter, melted and cooled
1⅓ cups (260g) granulated sugar
1 large egg + 1 egg yolk
1 tsp vanilla extract
½ tsp lemon juice or white vinegar
1½ cups (200g) all-purpose flour
2 tbsp (10g) cocoa powder
Strong red food coloring (the amount depends on how bright you want your brownies to be)
7 tbsp (100g) white chocolate chips

FOR THE CREAM CHEESE FROSTING
4 tbsp (60g) unsalted butter, softened
3¾oz (110g) cream cheese
1 tsp vanilla extract
2 cups (250g) powdered sugar, sifted

01 Preheat the oven to 350°F/180°C (160°C fan)/Gas mark 4 and line an 8in (20cm) square baking pan with parchment paper (see page 16).

02 To make the brownies, put the melted butter and sugar into a large mixing bowl and beat together with an electric hand mixer until light and fluffy. Add the egg, egg yolk, vanilla extract and lemon juice or vinegar and continue to beat until the mixture thickens. Add the flour, cocoa powder and red food coloring and fold in with a wooden spoon or rubber spatula until combined, then fold in the chocolate chips until evenly distributed.

03 Scoop the batter into your prepared pan and smooth it out evenly with the back of a spoon, then bake for about 30 minutes, or until crisp on top and the middle no longer wobbles. Leave to cool completely in the pan.

04 When the brownie is cool, make the frosting. Put the softened butter into a large mixing bowl and beat with an electric whisk until smooth and creamy. Add the cream cheese and vanilla extract and beat again until no lumps remain. Gradually add the sifted icing sugar, beating with each addition until fully combined.

05 Spoon the frosting onto the brownie and smooth it out evenly with a metal spatula, then cut into 16 squares. Enjoy!

06 Store in an airtight container in the refrigerator for up to 5 days.

HOT CHOCOLATE PUDDING

Serves 6-8

~~

Calling all chocolate lovers: this pudding is for you! A super-soft, warm chocolate sponge with a silky, rich hot chocolate sauce that starts at the top and gradually makes its way to the bottom while cooking, this pudding is the luxury you didn't know you needed. What's more, it's incredibly easy to make, making it perfect for dinner parties when you want to serve something warm and indulgent after your main meal.

50 minutes

FOR THE CAKE BATTER

Scant 1 cup (125g) all-
  purpose flour
½ cup (100g) superfine
  sugar
5 tsp (25g) cocoa powder
2 tsp baking powder
½ tsp salt
4 tbsp (60g) unsalted
  butter, melted and cooled
¾ cup (175ml) milk

FOR THE SAUCE

⅓ cup (80g) superfine
  sugar
½ cup (100g) light brown
  sugar
¼ cup (20g) cocoa powder
1¼ cups (300ml) boiling
  water

01 Preheat the oven to 350°F/180°C (160°C fan)/Gas mark 4 and grease a deep 11 x 7in (28 x 18cm) ovenproof dish with butter.

02 To make the cake batter, put the flour, sugar, cocoa powder, baking powder and salt into a large mixing bowl and stir together with a balloon whisk. Pour in the melted butter and milk and mix together until completely combined. Scoop the batter into the prepared dish and smooth it out evenly with the back of the spoon.

03 To make the sauce, in a separate medium bowl, mix together the sugars and cocoa powder until combined, then sprinkle over the cake batter (it will look like a lot of mixture).

04 Carefully pour the boiling water into the dish. Do not mix or stir it in, just let it sit on the top.

05 Carefully transfer the dish to the oven and bake for about 35 minutes until the cake is crisp and cracked on top. Leave to cool for a few minutes before serving. Enjoy!

FUDGY CHOCOLATE CHIP BLONDIES

Makes 16

~~

These blondies are super fudgy and packed with chocolate pieces. They're basically a white chocolate brownie, so if you love white chocolate as much as I do, you will adore them. There's a reason this is one of my most popular recipes!

**40 minutes
+ 3 hours chilling**

8oz (225g) white chocolate, broken into pieces

8 tbsp (115g) unsalted butter

2 large eggs

5½ tbsp (70g) granulated sugar

2 tsp vanilla extract

1 cup + 3 tbsp (155g) all-purpose flour

1 tsp salt

⅔ cup (150g) white and milk chocolate chips (or find a chocolate bar with both; I like Kinder)

3 tbsp (60g) chocolate-hazelnut spread (I use Nutella)

SWAP:

~~

Use speculoos spread or peanut butter instead of the chocolate spread to change up the flavor!

01   Preheat the oven to 340°F/170°C (150°C fan)/Gas mark 3½ and line an 8in (20cm) square baking pan with parchment paper (see page 16).

02   Put the white chocolate and butter into a microwave-safe bowl and microwave on high in 30-second bursts, stirring at each interval, until smooth and runny. Leave to cool for 10 minutes while you continue with the next steps.

03   In a large mixing bowl, beat the eggs with an electric hand mixer until light and foamy (this can take 5–10 minutes), then beat in the sugar and vanilla extract until combined. Pour in the white chocolate mixture and beat until completely combined.

04   Sift in the flour and salt, then fold in with a wooden spoon or rubber spatula. Add the chocolate chips or chocolate bar pieces and fold in until evenly distributed. Scoop the batter into your prepared pan and smooth it out to the edges.

05   Put the chocolate-hazelnut spread into a microwave-safe bowl and microwave on high in 20-second bursts, stirring at each interval, until smooth and runny, then drizzle in lines over the top of the blondie. Swirl the chocolate through the batter with a knife or skewer to create a pretty pattern.

06   Bake for 20–25 minutes until the edges are lightly golden and the middle no longer wobbles. Leave to cool completely in the pan, then chill in the refrigerator for at least 3 hours for a firmer texture and a cleaner cut. Cut into 16 squares and enjoy!

07   Store in an airtight container for up to 5 days.

CHOCOLATE CHIP COOKIE DOUGH BARS

Makes 16

~

These are like soft chocolate chip cookies, but in a bar form. They're quicker and easier to make than thick individual cookies, plus you don't need extra time to refrigerate the dough before baking. They're loaded with chocolate chips, with a sprinkle of sea salt on top. Eat them cold out of the refrigerator or warm them in the microwave for the ultimate gooey cookie bar – yum!

40 minutes

8oz (225g) unsalted butter, softened

Generous ¾ cup (150g) light brown sugar

6 tbsp (75g) granulated sugar

2 large eggs

1 tsp vanilla extract

Generous 2 cups (270g) all-purpose flour

1 tsp baking soda

1 tsp salt

1¾ cups (400g) milk or dark chocolate chips

Sprinkle of sea salt (optional)

01 Preheat the oven to 350°F/180°C (160°C fan)/Gas mark 4 and line an 8 x 10in (20 x 25cm) baking pan with parchment paper (see page 16).

02 Put the butter and both sugars into a large mixing bowl and beat together with an electric hand mixer until light and fluffy. Add the eggs and vanilla extract and mix together with a wooden spoon until just combined. Fold in the flour, baking soda and salt until only a few streaks of flour remain, then fold in 1½ cups (350g) of the chocolate chips until evenly distributed.

03 Scoop the cookie dough into your prepared pan and smooth it out to the edges, then press the remaining chocolate chips into the top.

04 Bake for 20–25 minutes until the edges and top are golden, but there is still a very slight wobble in the middle. Remove from the oven and, while still warm, sprinkle over the sea salt, if using (this is optional but recommended!). Leave to cool completely in the pan, then cut into 16 bars.

05 These are best eaten on the day of baking or the day after, but can be stored in an airtight container at room temperature or in the refrigerator for up to 5 days. Feel free to reheat the bars to make them warm and gooey again.

FUDGY TRIPLE CHOCOLATE BROWNIES

Makes 16

~~

These brownies are the some of the best I've ever made. They're super rich and fudgy, with chewy edges and a crackly top. They are loaded with milk, white and dark chocolate chips, but feel free to add any extras, like nuts, chunks of your favorite chocolate bar or broken cream-filled chocolate sandwich cookies.

50 minutes + overnight chilling

6oz (170g) unsalted butter, melted and cooled
½ cup (100g) light brown sugar
¾ cup (150g) superfine sugar
2 large eggs
4.5oz (125g) dark chocolate (at least 50% cocoa/cacao), broken into pieces, melted and cooled (see page 17)
¾ cup (100g) all-purpose flour
6 tsp (30g) cocoa powder
1 tsp salt
7 tbsp (100g) dark chocolate chips
7 tbsp (100g) white chocolate chips
7 tbsp (100g) milk chocolate chips

01 Preheat the oven to 375°F/190°C (170°C fan)/Gas mark 5 and line an 8in (20cm) square baking pan with parchment paper (see page 16).

02 Put the melted butter and both sugars into a large mixing bowl and beat together with an electric hand mixer for about 2–3 minutes until fully combined and no lumps remain. Add the eggs and continue to beat until soft peaks form (this could take from a few minutes up to 15 minutes, depending on the temperature of the ingredients and your equipment). Mix in the melted chocolate until just combined.

03 Sift in the flour, cocoa powder and salt, then gently fold in with a wooden spoon or rubber spatula until just a few streaks of flour remain, keeping as much air in the mix as possible. Finally, fold in all the chocolate chips until evenly distributed and no streaks of flour remain.

04 Scoop the batter into your prepared pan and smooth it out evenly with the back of a spoon.

05 Bake for 25–30 minutes until the edges are cracked and the middle no longer wobbles. Leave to cool completely in the pan, then chill in the refrigerator overnight for best results. Cut into 16 squares and enjoy!

06 Store in an airtight container at room temperature or in the refrigerator for up to 5 days.

LEMONIES

Makes 16

~~

These lemonies have all the gorgeous, zesty flavors of a lemon drizzle cake with a fudgy texture. They're bursting with tangy lemon, with a fresh, sugary glaze on the top, which is definitely a must for me when it comes to anything lemon. They are easy to make and bake, and ideal for a relaxed, sunny day. Enjoy them at an afternoon tea or picnic, or even pop them into lunchboxes. Everyone will love them, so you may want to think about hiding them if you want them to last!

45 minutes

7.5oz (215g) unsalted
  butter, softened
Scant 1 cup (180g)
  granulated sugar
1 large egg + 1 egg yolk
4 tbsp (60ml) fresh lemon
  juice (about 1½ lemons)
2⅓ cups + 5 tbsp (300g)
  all-purpose flour
½ tsp baking powder
½ tsp salt
Grated zest of 1 lemon

FOR THE GLAZE

Generous 2 cups (250g)
  powdered sugar
5–6 tbsp lemon juice

01 Preheat the oven to 340°F/170°C (150°C fan)/Gas mark 3½ and line an 8in (20cm) square baking pan with parchment paper (see page 16).

02 Put the butter and sugar into a large mixing bowl and beat together with an electric hand mixer until light and fluffy. Add the egg, egg yolk and lemon juice and beat in until just combined. Sift in the flour, baking powder and salt, then fold in with a wooden spoon or rubber spatula. Fold in the lemon zest. The batter should resemble a cookie dough.

03 Spoon the batter into your prepared pan and smooth it out to the edges, then bake for 30–35 minutes until the top is crisp and light golden brown.

04 Meanwhile, make the glaze. In a small bowl, mix together the powdered sugar and lemon juice until runny and smooth.

05 Remove the lemonie from the oven and immediately pour over the glaze, then leave to cool completely in the pan. Cut into 16 squares and enjoy!

06 Store in an airtight container for up to 5 days.

CINNAMON SWIRL BANANA BREAD

Makes 10 slices

~~

This is one of my favorite recipes in the book. I make any excuse to bake it – birthdays, weddings, Christmas, a sunny day, a rainy day... Got a new fish? Let's make banana bread! I cannot get enough. Packed with banana flavor, the buttery cinnamon swirl adds moistness and creates the most amazing sugary crust on top. As you can tell, I'm very excited about this recipe, so if cinnamon and banana bread are your favorites, you will love it too!

1 hour 20 minutes

Scant 1 cup (225ml) vegetable oil
½ cup (100g) granulated sugar
½ cup (100g) light brown sugar
2 large eggs
2 tsp vanilla extract
2 cups (250g) all-purpose flour
1 tsp baking soda
¼ tsp salt
4 medium ripe bananas, mashed

FOR THE SWIRL

4 tbsp (60g) unsalted butter, melted
3½ tbsp (40g) dark brown sugar
3½ tbsp (40g) granulated sugar
2 tbsp ground cinnamon

01   Preheat the oven to 350°F/180°C (160°C fan)/Gas mark 4 and line a 9 x 5in (23 x 13cm) loaf pan with parchment paper or a loaf liner.

02   To make the cake batter, put the vegetable oil and both sugars into a large mixing bowl and mix together with a balloon whisk until combined, then mix in the eggs and vanilla extract until just combined. Sift in the flour, baking soda and salt, then fold in with a wooden spoon or rubber spatula until only a few streaks of flour remain. Fold in the mashed bananas until just combined.

03   To make the cinnamon swirl, in a small bowl, mix together all the ingredients using small spoon or a fork. It should be nice and thick.

04   Spread one quarter of the cake batter into the prepared loaf pan, then dollop over one quarter of the cinnamon mixture and swirl it through the batter with a knife or skewer. Repeat with the remaining batter and cinnamon swirl to make 3 more layers, finishing with the cinnamon swirl on the top.

05   Bake for 50–65 minutes until a toothpick inserted into the middle comes out clean. Leave to cool in the pan for at least 1 hour, then transfer to a cooling rack to cool completely. Cut into 10 slices to serve.

06   Store in an airtight container for up to 4 days. For extra sweetness, mix 3.5oz (100g) icing sugar with 4 tbsp boiling water, and drizzle over the banana bread before serving.

NO-BAKE SPECULOOS CHEESECAKE

Serves 12

This is one of my most popular recipes! When I first shared it, I received hundreds of messages and photos from people who had tried it. It has a buttery speculoos cookie base, a rich and creamy speculoos filling, and a speculoos spread topping. It's full of sweet, caramelized cookie flavors and is really easy to make. There's no baking involved, you just have to be patient while it sets... it's worth it, I promise!

30 minutes + 7 hours chilling

FOR THE BASE

9oz (250g) speculoos cookies (I use Biscoff)
5 tbsp (75g) unsalted butter, melted

FOR THE FILLING

1 cup (250ml) heavy cream
¼ cup sour cream
1lb (500g) full-fat cream cheese, at room temperature
6½ tbsp (50g) powdered sugar
1 tsp vanilla extract
Generous 1 cup (250g) speculoos spread/cookie butter (I use Biscoff)

FOR THE TOPPING

⅔ cup (150g) speculoos spread
3 speculoos cookies, 2 crushed + 1 left whole

01 Line the bottom of an 8in (20cm) round springform cake pan with a circle of parchment paper (see page 16).

02 To make the base, put the cookies into a food processor and process until finely crushed. Alternatively, put them into a plastic bag and crush with a rolling pin. Tip into a medium bowl, then pour in the melted butter and mix together with a spoon until fully combined. Press the mixture firmly into the bottom of your prepared cake pan with your hands or the back of the spoon, then pop into the refrigerator while you make the filling.

03 In a large mixing bowl, whip the heavy cream and sour cream with an electric hand mixer until stiff peaks form. In a separate bowl, beat together the cream cheese, powdered sugar, vanilla extract and speculoos spread with the electric mixer until smooth and creamy, then fold in the whipped cream with a rubber spatula until completely combined.

04 Remove the chilled base from the refrigerator, then spoon in the filling, smoothing it out to the edges and pressing it down onto the base to avoid any gaps. Chill in the refrigerator for at least 6 hours, or overnight, if possible, until completely set.

Recipe continued on next page...

05 When ready to decorate, put the speculoos spread for the topping into a microwave-safe bowl and microwave on high in 20-second bursts, stirring at each interval, until runny and smooth. Leave to cool slightly.

06 Remove the cheesecake from the pan and transfer to a cooling rack. Pour over half of the melted speculoos spread, smoothing it out and allowing it to drip over the edge, then repeat with the remaining spread for a really smooth, glossy topping. Sprinkle the crushed cookies around the edge, then place a whole cookie in the middle. Return to the refrigerator for at least 1 hour to set the topping before serving. Enjoy!

07 Store in the refrigerator for up to 3 days.

COOKIE DOUGH BROWNIES

Makes 16
~~

When you can't decide between cookies and brownies... These brownies are thick, fudgy and chocolatey, packed with big chunks of cookie dough and lots of chocolate chips. Both the brownie batter and cookie dough are super quick and easy to make, then you just throw them together. This is one of my most popular recipes and it's one of my favorite tray bakes.

50 minutes
+ 2 hours chilling

FOR THE BROWNIE BATTER
6oz (170g) unsalted butter, melted and cooled
1¼ cups (250g) superfine sugar
2 large eggs
4.5oz (125g) dark chocolate (at least 50% cocoa/cacao), melted and cooled (see page 17)
¾ cup (100g) all-purpose flour
6 tbsp (30g) cocoa powder
1 tsp salt
6 tbsp (80g) milk or dark chocolate chips

FOR THE COOKIE DOUGH
5 tbsp (70g) unsalted butter, softened
Scant ½ cup (90g) light brown sugar
1 egg yolk
1 tsp vanilla extract
Scant ⅔ cup (80g) all-purpose flour
½ tsp baking powder
⅓ cup (70g) milk or dark chocolate chips + extra for the topping

01   Preheat the oven to 375°F/190°C (170°C fan)/Gas mark 5 and line an 8in (20cm) square baking pan with parchment paper (see page 16).

02   First, make the brownie batter. Put the melted butter and sugar into a large mixing bowl and beat together with an electric hand mixer until completely combined. Add the eggs and continue to beat until the mixture is super thick, fluffy and pale, and has at least doubled in volume. Mix in the melted dark chocolate until combined.

03   Sift in the flour, cocoa powder and salt, then fold in with a wooden spoon or rubber spatula until just combined. Fold in the chocolate chips until evenly distributed. Set aside while you make the cookie dough.

04   To make the cookie dough, put the softened butter and brown sugar into a large mixing bowl and beat together with an electric hand mixer until light and fluffy. Add the egg yolk and vanilla extract and beat until just combined. Fold in the flour and baking powder with a wooden spoon or rubber spatula until just a few streaks of flour remain, then fold in the chocolate chips until evenly distributed.

05   Scoop the brownie batter into your prepared pan and smooth out evenly with the back of a spoon.

Recipe continued on next page...

241

06   Scoop up about half a tablespoon of cookie dough and roll into a small ball with your hands, then repeat with the remaining dough. Arrange the balls randomly over the top of the brownie batter, leaving gaps in between. Sprinkle over the extra chocolate chips.

07   Bake for 30 minutes until the edges are cracked and the cookie dough is golden brown and no longer wobbles in the middle. Leave to cool completely in the pan.

08   Chill in the refrigerator for at least 2 hours, or overnight, if possible, for a firmer texture and a cleaner cut. Cut into 16 squares and enjoy!

09   Store in an airtight container at room temperature or in the refrigerator for up to 1 week.

TIP:

If you don't want to make the brownie and cookie dough from scratch, feel free to use box mixes from the supermarket.

NO-BAKE WHITE CHOCOLATE CHEESECAKE

Serves 12

~

If you love white chocolate, this is the cheesecake for you. It's sweet and creamy, and absolutely delicious. Plus, there's no baking involved. It has a buttery shortbread base, a white chocolate cheesecake filling and a white chocolate ganache topping.

50 minutes + 8 hours chilling

FOR THE BASE
10oz (280g) shortbread cookies
5 tbsp (70g) unsalted butter, melted

FOR THE FILLING
1 cup (250ml) heavy cream
¼ cup sour cream
1lb (500g) cold full-fat cream cheese
1 cup (120g) powdered sugar
9oz (250g) white chocolate, melted and cooled to room temperature (see page 17)

FOR THE TOPPING
10.5oz (300g) white chocolate, in chunks + 1 square for the top
⅔ cup (140ml) heavy cream
1 tbsp unsalted butter
1½ tbsp (10g) shortbread cookie crumbs

01 Line the bottom of an 8in (20cm) round springform cake pan with a circle of parchment paper (see page 16).

02 To make the base, put the shortbread into a food processor and process until finely crushed. Alternatively, put them into a plastic bag and crush with a rolling pin. Tip into a large mixing bowl, then pour in the melted butter and mix with a spoon until fully combined. Press the mixture firmly into the bottom of your prepared pan with the back of a spoon, then pop into the refrigerator while you make the filling.

03 To make the filling, in a large mixing bowl, whip the heavy cream and sour cream with an electric hand mixer until stiff peaks form. In a separate large bowl, beat together the cream cheese and powdered sugar with the electric mixer until smooth. Pour in your melted white chocolate and mix fully, then fold in the whipped cream with a rubber spatula until just combined.

04 Remove the chilled base from the refrigerator, then spoon in the filling, smoothing it out to the edges and pressing it down onto the base to avoid any gaps. Chill in the refrigerator for at least 6 hours, or overnight, if possible, until completely set.

05 When ready to decorate, put the chocolate chunks, cream and butter for the topping into a microwave-safe bowl and microwave on high for 1 minute 20 seconds (the cream should be warm enough to melt the chocolate and butter without boiling and curdling). Leave to stand for about 2 minutes, then stir until the cream, butter and chocolate start to come together. Continue to stir until smooth and creamy. If the ganache is too runny, pop it in the refrigerator for 20 minutes to help it thicken.

SWAP:

~~

Use graham
crackers instead
of shortbread and
increase the
amount of butter
to 6oz (180g).

06 Remove the cheesecake from the pan and transfer to a
    cooling rack. Pour over the ganache, allowing it to drip over
    the edge. Quickly smooth the top using a metal spatula
    or the back of a spoon. Chill in the refrigerator for at least
    2 hours to set the ganache. Sprinkle the shortbread crumbs
    around the edge and place the square of chocolate in the
    middle. Cut into 12 slices to serve.

07 Store in the refrigerator for up to 3 days.

CINNAMON APPLE CAKE

Makes 10-16 pieces

~~

One of my favorite cake recipes. Moist, packed with juicy apples and a buttery cinnamon swirl, and topped with a sweet, sugary glaze, it tastes like a juicy cinnamon roll, but in cake form, and, dare I say it, I might prefer it to cinnamon rolls (and trust me, I LOVE cinnamon rolls). It's also quicker and easier to make. I hope you'll love it too!

1 hour

FOR THE APPLES

3½ tbsp (45g) granulated
   sugar
1 tsp ground cinnamon
2 apples, peeled, cored
   and diced

FOR THE CINNAMON SWIRL

¾ cup (150g) light brown
   sugar
2 tbsp ground cinnamon
8½ tbsp (120g) unsalted
   butter, melted

FOR THE CAKE BATTER

2¾ cups (360g) all-
   purpose flour
1 cup (200g) superfine
   sugar
4 tsp baking powder
1¼ cups (300ml) whole
   milk, at room temperature
1 tsp vanilla extract
2 large eggs, lightly beaten
7½ tbsp (110g) unsalted
   butter, melted and cooled
   slightly

FOR THE GLAZE

1⅔ cups (200g) powdered
   sugar
2 tbsp + 2 tsp (40ml) milk

01   Preheat the oven to 350°F/180°C (160°C fan)/Gas mark 4 and line an 8 x 10in (20 x 25cm) baking pan with parchment paper (see page 16).

02   First, prepare the apples. Put the sugar and the cinnamon into a small bowl and mix together with a spoon, then add the diced apples and stir until completely coated. Set aside.

03   Next, make the cinnamon swirl. Put the sugar, cinnamon and butter into a small bowl and mix with a spoon, then set aside.

04   To make the cake batter, put the flour, sugar and baking powder into a large mixing bowl and mix together with a balloon whisk until combined. Add the milk, vanilla extract and eggs and mix until just combined, then gently stir in the melted butter with a wooden spoon or rubber spatula.

05   Fold in the prepared apples, then pour the batter into your prepared pan, spreading it out to the edges. Dollop on the cinnamon swirl mixture, then using a knife or a skewer, swirl it through the batter (it should sit on the top rather than sink in).

06   Bake for 40–45 minutes until a toothpick inserted into the middle comes out mostly clean, with only a few crumbs or gooey cinnamon swirl, rather than wet cake batter.

07   While the cake is baking, make the glaze. In a small bowl, mix together the powdered sugar and milk with a spoon until smooth and runny. Remove the cake from the oven, then pour over the glaze and smooth it over the top. Leave to cool for at least 45 minutes in the pan, then remove and cut into 16–20 pieces. Enjoy warm or cold.

08   Store in an airtight container for up to 3 days.

CHEWY CHOCOLATE CHIP COOKIES

Makes about 16

~

These cookies are my favorite. I thought I preferred thick and gooey cookies, but after making these, my opinion changed. They are easy to make and absolutely delicious, with crisp, chewy, caramelized edges and soft centers, and loaded with chocolate chips. Feel free to use milk, white or dark chocolate chips to suit your taste buds.

50 minutes
+ 30 minutes chilling

7½ tbsp (110g) unsalted butter, melted and cooled
¾ cup (150g) light brown sugar
Generous ½ cup (115g) granulated sugar
1 large egg
1 tsp vanilla extract
1⅓ cups (180g) all-purpose flour
½ tsp baking soda
½ tsp salt
Scant 1 cup (200g) milk, white or dark chocolate chips

01   Preheat the oven to 350°F/180°C (160°C fan)/Gas mark 4.

02   Put the melted butter and both sugars into a large mixing bowl and mix together with a balloon whisk until the mixture starts to come away from the sides of the bowl and forms a smooth paste (this may take a few minutes). Add the egg and vanilla extract and stir until completely combined and smooth. The mixture should stay on the whisk for a few seconds before falling back into the bowl.

03   Sift in the flour, baking soda and salt, then gently fold in with a wooden spoon or rubber spatula until just a few streaks of flour remain. Fold in your chocolate chips until evenly distributed (there should be no streaks of flour remaining at this point). Cover the bowl with plastic wrap and chill in the refrigerator for at least 30 minutes.

04   Working in batches, scoop up about 1 tablespoon of the dough and place on a large nonstick cookie sheet (see page 11). Repeat to make about 6 cookies per batch, spacing them roughly 4in (10cm) apart.

05   Bake each batch of cookies in the oven for 8–10 minutes until the edges are crisp and golden brown. The cookies will look puffy when they come out of the oven, but will flatten and crinkle as they cool. Leave to cool on the sheet for about 20 minutes, then transfer to a cooling rack to cool completely. Enjoy!

06   Store in an airtight container for up to 4 days

INDEX

ACKNOWLEDGMENTS

~~

To every single one of my followers and friends on social media... thank you! Without you guys, I never would have written this book. Thank you for your constant support and love. I absolutely adore seeing you try my recipes, I love seeing you share them with your friends and family, and I hope they forever bring you joy.

Thank you to my amazing literary agents, Eve White and Ludo Cinelli. You guys have been incredible from the moment we first spoke about writing this book, when it was all 'just an idea'. You have been so supportive throughout the entire process and I couldn't have asked for more. Thank you also to Rachel Kenny for finding me on social media and having faith in me to actually write a book!

Thank you to Faith Mason for taking the most amazing photos for this book. You have really made my recipes come to life in the most beautiful way possible. Thank you to Katie Marshall for making every single one of the recipes in this book and making them look so, so delicious, and thank you to Faye Wears for sourcing the most perfect props. We had a lot of early mornings and long days, but I hope all the taste-testing made up for it.

Thank you to everyone at Ebury Press with a special mention to Laura Higginson for believing in the potential for this book and Emily Brickell, whose organisation skills are on another level. This book would have never come together so smoothly without you.

Thank you to the very talented Nikki Dupin and Emma Wells of Nic&Lou for the incredible design and super-cute drawings throughout the book. Page by page, you've brought together the most exciting, fun and colorful book, as I always imagined it would be.

Thank you to my fiancé Bernie, the other half of Fitwaffle and self-titled chief recipe tester. Bernie works behind the scenes of Fitwaffle and it wouldn't exist without him. Thank you for forever supporting me, helping me, guiding me and keeping me sane. I couldn't have done this without you.

Lastly, thank you to both of our families for forever supporting us in our crazy ventures!

Thank you all, Eloise x

weldon**owen**

an imprint of Insight Editions
P.O. Box 3088
San Rafael, CA 94912
www.weldonowen.com

CEO Raoul Goff
VP Publisher Roger Shaw
Project Editor Jourdan Plautz
VP Manufacturing Alix Nicholaeff
Production Manager Joshua Smith

Original edition first published by The Random House
Group Limited, London.

ISBN: 9781681889290

Manufactured in China by Insight Editions
10 9 8 7 6 5 4 3 2 1

ROOTS of PEACE   🌲 REPLANTED PAPER

Insight Editions, in association with Roots of Peace, will plant two trees
for each tree used in the manufacturing of this book. Roots of Peace is
an internationally renowned humanitarian organization dedicated to
eradicating land mines worldwide and converting war-torn lands into
productive farms and wildlife habitats. Roots of Peace will plant two
million fruit and nut trees in Afghanistan and provide farmers there with
the skills and support necessary for sustainable land use.